Library of
Davidson College

# RELIGION AND RATIONAL CHOICE

# LIBRARY OF PHILOSOPHY AND RELIGION

General Editor: John Hick, H. G. Wood
Professor of Theology, University of Birmingham

This new series of books will explore contemporary religious understandings of man and the universe. The books will be contributions to various aspects of the continuing dialogues between religion and philosophy, between scepticism and faith, and between the different religions and ideologies. The authors will represent a correspondingly wide range of viewpoints. Some of the books in the series will be written for the general educated public and others for a more specialised philosophical or theological readership.

*Already published*

| | |
|---|---|
| William H. Austin | THE RELEVANCE OF NATURAL SCIENCE TO THEOLOGY |
| Paul Badham | CHRISTIAN BELIEFS ABOUT LIFE AFTER DEATH |
| Patrick Burke | THE FRAGILE UNIVERSE |
| William Lane Craig | THE *KALAM* COSMOLOGICAL ARGUMENT |
| | THE COSMOLOGICAL ARGUMENT FROM PLATO TO LEIBNIZ |
| Lynn A. de Silva | THE PROBLEM OF THE SELF IN BUDDHISM AND CHRISTIANITY |
| Padmasiri de Silva | AN INTRODUCTION TO BUDDHIST PSYCHOLOGY |
| Ramchandra Gandhi | THE AVAILABILITY OF RELIGIOUS IDEAS |
| J. C. A. Gaskin | HUME'S PHILOSOPHY OF RELIGION |
| H. A. Hodges | GOD BEYOND KNOWLEDGE |
| Hywel D. Lewis | PERSONS AND LIFE AFTER DEATH |
| Eric Lott | VEDANTIC APPROACHES TO GOD |
| Hugo A. Meynell | AN INTRODUCTION TO THE PHILOSOPHY OF BERNARD LONERGAN |
| F. C. T. Moore | THE PSYCHOLOGICAL BASIS OF MORALITY |
| Dennis Nineham | THE USE AND ABUSE OF THE BIBLE |
| Bernard M. G. Reardon | HEGEL'S PHILOSOPHY OF RELIGION |
| John J. Shepherd | EXPERIENCE, INFERENCE AND GOD |
| Patrick Sherry | RELIGION, TRUTH AND LANGUAGE-GAMES |
| Robert Young | FREEDOM, RESPONSIBILITY AND GOD |

*Further titles in preparation*

# RELIGION AND RATIONAL CHOICE

Shivesh Chandra Thakur

Barnes & Noble Books
Totowa, New Jersey

© Shivesh Chandra Thakur 1981

All rights reserved. No part of this publication may be reproduced or transmitted, in any form or by any means, without permission

*First published 1981 by*
THE MACMILLAN PRESS LTD
*London and Basingstoke
Companies and representatives
throughout the world*

Macmillan ISBN 0–333–27419–9

*First published in the USA 1981 by*
BARNES & NOBLE BOOKS
*81 Adams Drive
Totowa, New Jersey, 07512*
Barnes & Noble ISBN 0–389–20047–6

*Printed in Hong Kong*

To My Mother

# Contents

| | |
|---|---|
| *Preface* | ix |
| 1 Introduction | 1 |
| 2 Religion Without God | 10 |
| 3 Towards a Definition | 21 |
| 4 Religion and Religions | 33 |
| 5 Does Religion Explain? | 47 |
| 6 Believing and Understanding | 60 |
| 7 Religious Language and Truth | 70 |
| 8 Science, Magic and Religion | 83 |
| 9 The Rejection of Religious Belief | 95 |
| 10 Religion and Rational Choice | 105 |
| *Notes* | 116 |
| *Index* | 121 |

# Preface

Since religion has been a much discussed subject for so long, any book about it now can, strictly speaking, only be a new way of putting together what is already known. That is certainly true of this book on philosophy of religion. The sources of the existing ideas have, wherever possible, been acknowledged in the text. All that remains for me to do now is to thank the authors concerned, and also the many whose ideas, while not specifically used here, have none the less helped shape my thinking on the subject. It is to be hoped that the use made here of these ideas contributes towards an increased understanding of religion.

I am indebted to numerous individuals – teachers and students of philosophy and religion – who have helped with discussion and criticism of themes in this book. I am especially grateful, however, to the following: Professor John Hick for including it in his series and for valuable comments on an earlier draft of the book; Professors D. J. O'Connor and H. D. Lewis and Mr Renford Bambrough for encouraging me to undertake the writing of the book (Mr Bambrough also commented on an earlier draft); Professor David Hamlyn for criticism of part of the draft; Professor Ninian Smart for constant encouragement and for comments on the draft; and Professor Heinz Walz and Mrs Rosemary Walz for their warm hospitality and support while I wrote parts of the draft. I also express my thanks to my secretary, Miss Helen Newman, for patiently preparing the typescript.

Finally, I express my love and grateful thanks to my children – Sunita, Ravi and Sanjay – whose affection and enthusiasm kept me going.

*Guildford 1979*              SHIVESH CHANDRA THAKUR

# 1 Introduction

Frank Ramsey declared, as early as 1925, that there was nothing to discuss: there was 'no discussable subject (of the first order)';[1] at least not in philosophy. This was, of course, the outcome of the philosophical climate created by positivist claims and some of the assertions of Russell and early Wittgenstein. Positivism, mainly through its verificationist theory of meaning, held that the only significant statements were those made by science; the rest were either nonsensical or else pseudo-statements expressing emotional and other personal attitudes of the speaker, e.g. ethical statements. Early linguistic philosophy, led by Wittgenstein, himself influenced in important ways by the spirit of positivism, regarded traditional philosophical problems like freedom and determinism, the body–mind problem and that of the existence of God as puzzles arising from linguistic confusion. Careful analysis of linguistic idiom would soon either dissolve them or else show them to belong to the sphere of one or other science – physics, mathematics, logic or some other. Metaphysics in particular was simply the product of 'bewitchment of the intellect' brought about by the arbitrary and colourful but misleading use of words. The job of a philosopher was to show the fly 'the way out of the fly-bottle'. If all this was true, then, of course, philosophy had no autonomous domain of its own: it either folded itself up altogether or tried to show how one or another of its traditional problems, the so-called perennial ones, did not really exist at all. Certainly there was nothing very significant or useful for philosophy to discuss. At least ethics and theology, two of the traditionally important branches of philosophy, had no subject matter left; for according to Ramsey, 'the objectivity of good was a thing we had settled and dismissed with the existence of God. Theology and Absolute Ethics are two famous subjects which we have realised to have no real objects.'[2] But Ramsey, like many other prophets, had failed to notice the irony in his claim. Given the stuff of which philosophers are made and the fact that there were going to be a few of them around, even if there was nothing else to discuss, one could rely on them to go on discussing why there was nothing to discuss: that there were no first-order subjects was not going to deter them. The amount of published literature alone in the last fifty years bears ample testimony to that. It is not strictly relevant here that some of it has been eminently worthwhile also, and in many different ways.

Posterity has evidently not agreed with Ramsey, and perhaps fortunately so. But even those philosophers who did, or would, refuse to join him in a communal suicide have often tended to be more sympathetic to the somewhat restricted claim that there was nothing for philosophers to discuss about religion This sympathy has been based on many different grounds, the more noteworthy among them being the following:

1. There can be nothing *worth* discussing about religion, for once the philosopher's cold stare is directed, hard and straight, on religion, the latter dissolves into nothing, like the beguiling nymph in Keats' *Lamia*. The critical analysis of religious claims shows them to be either a collection of meaningless utterances or a bag of superstitions. Apart from those of them that sometimes provided the useful moral fabric of societies, the rest were either nonsensical or false. This kind of reasoning, expressed in somewhat varying terminology, has a rather distinguished ancestry and includes such names as Hume, Feuerbach, Marx, Freud, Ayer and Flew.

2. More interestingly, even paradoxically, the claim is made by philosophers, not otherwise unsympathetic to religion, that philosophy is not entitled to apply its usual technique of rational analysis and criticism to religious utterances. For religion, it is argued, is not the sphere of reason but of faith; and to apply criteria of judgment borrowed from one sphere to another quite unlike the first is not only inappropriate but downright disingenuous. And since discussion, properly so-called, can only be in rational terms, it follows that there can, strictly speaking, be nothing to discuss about religion, not philosophically anyway. Not only do philosophers like Wittgenstein, Winch, Phillips, Prior and Hughes subscribe in somewhat different ways to this view but even theologians have supported it.

3. To these should be added the conclusion entailed by the claims of mystics regarding the ineffability of the 'reality' encountered in religious experience. The object of religious attitudes, it is claimed, can be experienced or intuited but not rationally

discussed. It is not just that religion happens to be the sphere of faith, and not of rationality; the 'reality' of religion transcends or defies reason altogether. Rational enquiry as a means of apprehension of this reality is not only inadequate but perhaps even perverse.

These claims, if true, may, at first sight, seem to have the rather undisturbing conclusion that there can be no philosophy of religion. But since it is the prerogative of philosophy, by and large, to apply and devise criteria of intelligibility, rationality, coherence, truth, existence, value and the like; and since our ability to determine these in relation to the concepts used and claims made in any sphere of human activity is deemed essential to our understanding of that activity, it would seem that if there is no philosophy of religion, we fail in very important respects to have a proper understanding of religion. Put this way, the prospect is disturbing, or should be, at least to those who regard religion as one of the most important endeavours of man, certainly comparable to and perhaps surpassing in importance science, technology and certain very potent specimens of political ideology. Even among sceptics, agnostics, atheists and those that are uncompromisingly irreligious, there are few who have disputed the power of religion as a force in human history, be it for good or evil. And what is more, religion as a phenomenon does not seem to be showing any signs of breathing its last, even though institutionalised forms of it may be on the wane.

In view of this, any fresh attempt at the formulation of the outlines of a philosophy of religion cannot be dismissed *a priori* as unworthy of serious consideration despite the views of the positivists, fideists and ineffabilists. But what must be the outline and contents of such a philosophy of religion? What criteria of adequacy and soundness must it satisfy? What questions must it discuss? What answers might it give to questions that are deemed legitimate? These are matters of such a high order of abstraction and complexity that the best to be hoped for is that the sequel might contain some hints. The question that cannot be postponed in this way, however, is how one sets about the task of outlining a philosophy of religion. Perhaps the Dodo's enlightening remark that the best way to explain a Caucus-Race is to do it, may give the most appropriate clue.

But this will not quite do – not yet, anyway. For, despite the difficulties raised by sceptics, fideists and the like, it is not as though there is not already enough philosophical literature on religion.

Quite the contrary. These groups of philosophers themselves have contributed handsomely to the philosophical discussion of religion, if only to make the point that such discussion was either impossible or unprofitable. So what is the point, it may be asked quite pertinently, of adding yet another volume on philosophy of religion?

Perhaps there is none at all. But it seems to me that most philosophical discussions of religion so far have been vitiated by one major fault. Accounts of religion, like almost all influential academic and other intellectual exercises in the last two or three centuries, have by and large been the work of Western scholars and intellectuals, often less familiar with, but sometimes simply disinclined to take seriously non-Western religious traditions. This claim needs important qualifications as soon as it is made and certainly requires elaboration. For it would be clear to anyone knowledgeable about the field that but for the painstaking and pioneering work of such figures as Max Müller, Sir William Jones and other eminent Europeans, many orientals would have remained relatively ignorant of their own religious and literary heritage. But these great scholars have seldom been theoreticians interested in conceptual and philosophical questions about religion. Besides, even they, like Western anthropologists studying esoteric cultures, did not, indeed could not, start with a clean slate. They carried with them European ideas and presuppositions about what religion was, or ought to be. Consequently, their work was characterised by a not-always subconscious bias which revealed itself in the kinds of questions asked and in the classification and categorisation of non-Western religious ideas and practices. There have been important exceptions; but by and large, I think, this has been the case, until relatively recently. Accounts of religion have, therefore, I maintain, tended to be somewhat parochial, failing to apply to, say, Eastern religions, not to mention so-called 'primitive' religions.

The concept of religion has not often been given either the breadth or clarity required. An indirect, but important, consequence of this lack of breadth has often resulted in the selection of problems and issues which rather than properly belonging to the philosophy of religion in general, have tended to be those of, say, Christian theology. To use somewhat technical terms, these accounts have been largely 'prescriptive', whereas what is needed for a perspicuous presentation of theoretical issues relating to religion is a 'descriptive' one, i.e., an account which will be true of at least the major living religions of the world, e.g. Hinduism,

Buddhism, Judaism, Christianity, Islam and their main schools or sects, if not of every single instance of what is recognised as religion.

While the main defect of available definitions of religion, in the present context, is that they delineate the concept rather narrowly, and that they are prescriptive, i.e. requiring, by implication, all forms of religion to fit a sort of conceptual strait-jacket, there are other shortcomings too. Many of them are unduly 'theocentric' or God-centred; excessively preoccupied with institutionalised religions and, therefore, missing a very important dimension reflected in the outlook of individuals whose religiosity is non-doctrinaire and personal, but truly religious none the less; and reductionist, that is, while professing to illuminate religion, end up dissolving it into something other than religion. Feuerbach, Marx and Freud are the outstanding names among reductionists, though there are a host of lesser figures, who, in a variety of ways, achieve a similar task.

In order to elucidate better what I have been saying of available accounts of religion, let me now discuss briefly some well-known definitions as random samples.[3] Let us start with James Martineau's definition of religion as 'the belief in an ever living God', for example. Apart from making the belief in God essential to the concept of religion, which I will argue later should not be done, it is clear too that this definition takes no account of aspects of religion other than belief, which are equally important, e.g. behaviour – ritual, moral and others – as well as attitudes which have traditionally been considered appropriate. On the other hand, Herbert Spencer's definition, that religion is the 'recognition that all things are manifestations of a power that transcends knowledge', while not strictly theocentric, tends to define a specific form of religion, namely the mystical; and in its suggestion that the power in question transcends knowledge, becomes prejudicial to the claims of those religions which assert that this 'power' can be known through special revelation and incarnation. The merit of this definition, however, is that it is more likely to accommodate the spirit of less formal and more subjective forms of belief. F. H. Bradley's 'religion as the attempt to express the complete reality of goodness', tends to identify religion with morality and, worse still, to a particular view of it. One can easily imagine those who would want to say that religion is not primarily, perhaps not at all, the attempt to express the complete reality of goodness: that it is one's response to whatever 'reality' may be. Besides, one should not *a priori* rule out of court possible forms of religion which may wish to express the complete reality, of, say, evil or wickedness.

Among examples of a somewhat different sort, there is J. M. E. McTaggart's account of religion 'as an emotion resting on the conviction of a harmony between ourselves and the world at large'. It is clear that this says too little, though what it says may be true. While emotion of the appropriate sort may be an important part of religion, it has to be more than that. Beliefs and behaviour of certain sorts must find mention. What is more, polytheistic forms of religion, and dualistic ones like Zoroastrianism, do not start from this assumption of harmony. On the contrary, they explicitly postulate inimical forces which need to be vanquished or subdued, and religiosity (or an important part of it) is a consequence of the attempt either to propitiate these forces themselves or else to befriend benign ones whose aid is required if we are to achieve harmony with the world at large. The harmony is a future possibility rather than a present fact. C. P. Tiele's 'religion as piety', would seem plainly to be question-begging, as indeed may Otto's account in terms of the 'holy'; for 'piety' and 'holiness' are terms which themselves cannot be understood except through a prior understanding of the concept, and context, of religion. Edward Caird's definition of religion as the 'expression of one's ultimate attitude to the universe', may have much to commend itself, for it is not unduly restrictive and captures what many would regard as describing what religion is about. It certainly accommodates quite well the essence of much of what I referred to earlier as non-institutionalised, personal forms of religiosity. But it does not, not explicitly anyway, incorporate the belief and action elements of religion; though it must in all fairness be added that the term 'expression' could easily be interpreted as 'expression through belief and action'. Until that is done, however, the definition would seem to remain inadequate.

We will now turn, again only briefly, to those accounts of religion which can be, and have been, seen as reductionist. I cited the names of Feuerbach, Marx and Freud in this connection; and since their treatment of religion is so well known, perhaps it is unnecessary to give details. I will, therefore, merely quote from D. Z. Phillips, who in his *Religion Without Explanation* discusses reductionist views of religion held by eminent social scientists:

> So far in discussing the accounts of religion offered by Frazer,

Tylor, Marett and Freud, what we have found is that, despite important differences, they have all been concerned with a conscious reductionism in their treatment of religious belief. At some stage or other they all attribute an error to the worshipper, the error of animism. Either because of his intellectual primitiveness, his emotional instability, or his unconscious desires, man projects into the outer world features of his own character. This notion of projection they owe to Ludwig Feuerbach.[4]

Quoting Kamenka, Phillips goes on to argue how Feuerbach himself was an inheritor of 'Hume's philosophical legacy'. It is ironical that Phillips himself, in my opinion, gives a reductionist account of religion.

What is wrong with such reductionist attempts is not that what they say is necessarily false. After all if religion is a human enterprise then quite understandably it must answer some of man's urges and needs, wishes and fantasies. What seems objectionable is the claim, explicit or implied, that because religion arose in answer to these needs, etc, it must be a form of self-delusion, to be cast away at the dawn of 'wisdom'. There seems to be no recognition whatever of the fact that according to many religions, a certain sort of religious vision or awakening is the highest, if not the only, form of wisdom; and when that happy event takes place, the outcome is not an inebriating irreligiosity but the heightening of one's conviction that merely human desires, needs and aspirations are at best traps and at worst irrelevancies. One does not have to accept without examination the truth of this claim any more than of the one which declares religion to be an illusion; but it must be recorded as a well-authenticated fact about religion. Science, and particularly technology, it may be argued plausibly, owes as much to our warmongering instincts as to anything else. The Greeks made impressive mathematical discoveries about projectiles because they needed to use them against their enemies; and in recent times a whole new revolutionary era, that of nuclear science and technology, was introduced and brought about by the Second World War. It is interesting, sometimes illuminating, to note these historical details. But these do not usually prompt us into concluding that science and technology are nothing in their own right. Nor do we try to write off scientific discoveries simply because they were made possible originally by some limited utilitarian goal. We admire Archimedes' Law for its own sake and for what it allows us to do and seldom bemoan the fact that his great discovery was made in the course of an attempt to find out whether a goldsmith was cheating the member of the nobility on whose behest Archimedes was acting. Likewise, Kepler's laws of planetary motion do not in the least cease to qualify as some of the most important scientific discoveries made by man, simply because these were made, almost inadvertently, in the course of his attempt to demonstrate the truth of a highly abstruse, Pythagorean, mystical belief, i.e. that planetary orbits, for example, could be shown to fit the five regular solids. It is particularly paradoxical that reductionist accounts of religion should owe largely to social scientists whose avowed aim is, or should be, to *describe* phenomena under investigation, no more no less.

For these reasons, it seems to me that the very first task a philosopher of religion must undertake is the formidable one of determining what religion is, descriptively. This is, of course, a demand for a definition, however loose. While I do not underestimate the difficulties or hazards involved in trying to formulate a single definition for the diverse manifestations of religion, I do believe that it is important to attempt one. For unless one knows, with a reasonable degree of clarity and without avoidable bias towards a particular specimen, what religion is, I do not see how the more specifically philosophical questions about religion can be profitably or adequately discussed. It is not, however, just in the context of a philosophy of religion that such a definition is important. 'Religion' is a term much used and much abused. Talk about religion, more than almost anything else, seems to be characterised, and determined, by an arbitrary selection of one or another of its many features as essential, often with a complete disregard for its other characteristics. Any attempt to restore the balance and thus bring clarity to an area of discourse not renowned for its perspicuity should, to my mind, be an exercise eminently worthwhile in its own right. Accordingly, the next three chapters of this book deal with the issue of definition. Chapter 2 prepares the ground for definition by arguing why the concept of God cannot be part of a general definition of religion; chapter 3 attempts to offer an actual definition; and chapter 4, while primarily assessing the soundness of the proposed definition, argues that the concept of religion does not presuppose a community or society of practitioners.

While the definition offered is intended as a proposal inviting scrutiny and comment by others better qualified than myself to judge on its accuracy and adequacy, the rest of the task of the book has to proceed on the assumption – sound, I hope – that the account of religion here offered is adequate and to the point, *and* descriptive. This assumption, or hope, provides the starting-point for the discussion of some of those philosophical issues that philosophers, and other students of religion, have seen as pertinent to the understanding of religion. I believe that the clarity in the concept of religion achieved through the definition will prove rewarding. For what can or cannot be said with regard to one or other philosophical issue relating to religion will henceforth be determined – partly at least – by the definition: the latter should mark the boundaries of discourse, to some extent anyway. I am convinced that such a corrective is specially required in the philosophy of religion. This is not to say that the philosophy of religion can now cease to be the application to religion of general philosophical views and theories, but merely to hope that the range of such application will be somewhat restricted by a clearer grasp of what religion is. It may, indeed will, still be possible to stretch the concept one way or another in order to foist on it a particular philosophical dogma or doctrine, but the incidence could, or should, decline. If I succeed in attaining my objectives in this book, then there should, on the one hand, be greater clarity about what religion is and, on the other, what philosophers, and to some extent, social scientists, may or may not legitimately say about it.

It is with this hope that chapters 5–10 try to come to grips with such questions as: Can religious belief-systems be regarded as explanatory theories? Is religion simply pseudo-science, or does it have a distinctive function of its own? How should one go about determining the meaning and truth of religious utterances? In what way, if any, can religion be distinguished from science and magic? Does the fact of the rejection of religious belief have any philosophical significance in the context of the questions above? What is the role of reason in religion? Does the adoption of 'the religious point of view' necessarily lead to ontological relativism of the worst sort? These are samples of the kinds of questions discussed, and not an exhaustive list of them. While it is hardly to be expected that the answers I give in the relevant chapters will appeal to everyone, it is certainly hoped that my approach will be judged to be interesting, and perhaps rewarding as well.

# 2 Religion Without God

To someone coming in from another culture what must seem striking about traditional philosophy of religion in the West is its excessive preoccupation with the concept of God, a personal supreme being. Pride of place has almost invariably been given to the issue of whether such a being exists. The familiar 'proofs' for the existence of God, starting with Aquinas's Five Ways, and the criticisms thereof have been so regularly ladled out as compulsory rations as to become tedious and unappetising. One would have thought that after centuries of endless and inconclusive debate over the issue, some obvious lessons would have been learnt; and at least modern philosophy of religion would have abandoned it as fruitless, if not misguided as well. But this does not seem to have been the case. The format of the debate often seems to be different, and old propositions are presented in new formulations. Also, there is evidence of a greater variety of logical and formal tools and techniques being employed. But the basic preoccupation with the concept of God remains. Even when other conceptual issues are tackled, as indeed they often are, for example, the nature of 'religious language', the question of truth in relation to claims made in religion, etc, it does not require too much sophistication to discern that the outcome of the debate about God's existence singularly predetermines, to a large extent, that of most other issues; except when the discussion is merely a semantic or logical squabble which could easily have been carried on in some other area of philosophy, notably epistemology or philosophical logic.

But the foregoing need not lead anyone, except the unwitting, to a conclusion either more ominous or more momentous than the somewhat trivial one that philosophy of religion too has been culturally determined. It is because the dominant forms of religion in the West have been God-centred that philosophers – apologists as well as sceptics – thinking about religion, have been unable to depart from this theocentrism, without running the risk of being accused of debating the merely inessential. In so far as it was philosophy of religion, rather than biblical theology, the appropriate thing would, of course, have been to take a wider view of religion, i.e. to start from an enlarged concept or religion, required, I would say, by the inclusion of certain non-Judaic forms. But this, for historical reasons, was not to be expected, until relatively recently. So the centrality of God, and the consequent need to devise and refute arguments for his existence, remained.

Historically, it is not hard to understand the motivation behind the attempt to demonstrate God's existence. What could be better and more important for any person of intellect to do than to establish rationally the existence of an entity which was accepted on faith anyway, and which was so central to the culture of the region? But with hindsight it is, or should be, evident that this exercise is (a) futile, (b) paradoxical, and (c) pointless, when the reference of religion has been extended to include 'non-Western' examples.

In view of what I have already said, I hope it will not be expected that I should devote any length of time discussing these 'proofs' or their refutations. But I feel that I owe an outline of the case showing their futility. It is generally recognised now, I think, that the only two serious contenders among these are the so-called ontological argument and the argument from design. In relation to the first of these, it is now widely agreed that Kant sounded the death-knell, at least to all traditional formulations of the argument, by showing that since existence is not a predicate, it cannot be a perfection either; and hence deducing the existence of God from the notion of 'the most perfect being' was an exercise comparable to producing something out of nothing, which one would be unlikely to accomplish unless one was God!

Norman Malcolm, however, has claimed that while one of Anselm's ontological arguments fails as proof, there is another which does not.[1] Malcolm recommends carefully distinguishing the first from the second, and tries to establish that the second one is sound as proof. The first argument fails, according to Malcolm, because it tries to deduce the existence of God from the concept of 'the most perfect being'. But the second derives God's existence from the notion that he is a 'necessary being', namely a being whose non-existence is impossible. Combining this with the first argument, Anselm claims (according to Malcolm) that, of course, 'the being whose non-existence is logically impossible' is greater than the one who merely *happens* to exist, so God must exist necessarily, i.e. 'It is necessary that God exists'; and 'God necessarily exists' entails 'God exists'. That 'God is a necessary being' seems to be embedded in the concept we supposedly have of him as unlimited and absolutely independent: nothing could prevent him from existing; he does not merely have duration but is eternal. Malcolm goes on to argue that Kant's, and other related, objections to the first of Anselm's arguments do not affect the second, for 'although it may be an error to regard existence as a property of things that have contingent existence, it does not follow that it is an error to regard necessary existence as a property of God'. According to Malcolm, those who think that necessary truths are merely linguistic conventions are right, but they are wrong in thinking that this implies that *all* existential propositions must be contingent; for common usage or linguistic conventions differ, and God's existence may yet be necessary.

While it is correct, Malcolm continues, to interpret 'A triangle has three angles' as a hypothetical proposition translatable as 'If a triangle exists, then it has three angles', 'God is a necessary being' cannot be interpreted in that way. For if we render 'God is a necessary being' as 'If God exists, then he necessarily exists', it would seem that the antecedent clause of the latter would have to imply that it is possible that God does not exist. But this involves a self-contradiction (not by itself but when we take the whole context). Kant and others agree, according to Malcolm, that 'God necessarily exists' is an *a priori* truth; and yet they also wish to maintain that it entails 'It is possible that he does not'; they cannot have it both ways.

For all the ingenuity of his reasoning, it nevertheless seems to me that Malcolm is guilty of the worst kind of question-begging. He agrees that it is an error to regard existence as a property of things that have contingent existence, but he insists that it need not be an error to regard necessary existence as a property of God. Since 'necessary' is an adjective qualifying the substantive 'existence', whatever applies essentially to the latter by itself must, one would have thought, apply to it even when qualified by the former; so that if 'existence' is not a property, 'necessary existence' cannot be so either. Nor does Malcolm seem to see the force of the Humean dictum that there can be no necessity about 'matters of fact'; and existence or non-existence being a matter of fact, all existence must be contingent only. Malcolm refuses, or simply fails, to see that 'If there existed an odd number between 7 and 9, it would exist necessarily, but it does not', is not in the least self-contradictory. In suggesting that Kant agrees that 'God necessarily exists' is *a priori*, I suspect that Malcolm may be confusing '*a priori*' with 'analytic', terms often hard to distinguish in practice but different all the same.

The ontological argument, on any interpretation, it seems to me, is bound to fail as proof, for it would in the end claim to have brought an entity into existence by a sheer fiat of definition. This, I feel, must also go for Plantinga's much more technical formulation of the argument, although I do not discuss its details here. Suffice it to say that Plantinga himself agrees with my conclusion. Having presented a 'modal version' of the argument and defended its soundness, he goes on to say:

> But here we must be careful; we must ask whether this argument is a successful piece of natural theology, whether it *proves* the existence of God. And the answer must be, I think, that it does not. An argument for God's existence may be *sound*, after all, without in any useful sense proving God's existence. Since I believe in God, I think the following argument is sound:
>
> > Either God exists or $7 + 5 = 14$
> > It is false that $7 + 5 = 14$
> > Therefore God exists.
>
> But obviously this isn't *proof*; no one who didn't already accept the conclusion would accept the first premise.[2]

As for the argument from design – which claims to show the existence of a designer or creator of the universe on the strength of the supposedly existing order or 'design' in the world – I am of the opinion that its merits as well as its limitations were convincingly brought out by Hume.[3] First of all, without a prior set of assumptions of certain sorts, it is not possible even to show that the world, as a whole, displays this supposed order, especially in view of the fact that for every fact allegedly providing evidence of order it is possible to cite another which does the opposite, e.g. floods, drought and other natural catastrophes, as against the regularity and precision with which day follows night and the seasons follow each other. Besides, it can be plausibly argued that we ought not to be excessively impressed with the amount of order there is in the world; much of it is presupposed by our very agreement to call it a 'world' or a 'universe', otherwise the term might have been 'chaos', if indeed the conditions for characterising it as anything whatsoever obtained. A certain amount of order is built into our convention of calling it a world or 'cosmos', and we ought not to claim 'extra mileage' for it, that is, of then reading it as evidence for a designer. But even if there were an impressive amount of order in evidence, it can be explained simply by the process of gradual evolution, as indeed happens to be the view taken by the relevant natural sciences. Or, why not postulate many gods at work? The order, when taken in conjunction with those states of affairs which point to a lack of it, is more likely to establish the existence of a designer or designers of limited power and ability than of a supreme God who creates the world out of nothing.

Earlier, I stated my view – shared, I believe, by other philosophers – that only the ontological argument and that from design deserve serious consideration as purported demonstrations of God's existence; and have, therefore, confined myself to the discussion of these so far. But the cosmological argument has its defenders, the most notable recent one being Craig who has devoted a whole book to the exegesis and defence of a particular version of this argument which he calls 'the *Kalām* cosmological argument'.[4] It is not possible here to undertake a fuller examination of the details of Craig's book, nor, given my general opinion of these arguments, should this be expected. But I doubt that the version of the cosmological argument that Craig is defending succeeds in overcoming the formidable difficulties it faces in establishing the existence of a single, personal, omnipotent God that were pointed out, say, by Russell in his debate with Copleston.[5] Its impotence as proof derives from the unsoundness of the logic that *any* form of cosmological argument must employ; and this position, I fear, is not altered by the *Kalām* version. Let me instantiate, briefly, what I mean. The *Kalām* version, according to Craig,[6] can be displayed syllogistically as follows:

1. Everything that begins to exist has a cause of its existence.
2. The universe began to exist.
3. Therefore, the universe has a cause of its existence.

Quite understandably, critics of the argument would deny the second premise by maintaining that there is nothing logically incoherent in supposing that the universe does not have a beginning in time. Indeed, Hinduism maintains that the cycle of periodic 'creation' and 'destruction' is quite literally eternal, and it is wrong to hold that the world 'began to exist'. Part at least of the reason for denying a beginning in time for the universe is that the supposition entails that at the time of the beginning, as it were, something would seem to have come out of nothing, a logical absurdity, which not even divine discretion (or indiscretion?) may be said to overcome. And I do not believe that the two arguments in support of this second premise that Craig puts forward (on page 65 of his book) are logically sound and hence succeed in accomplishing the job demanded of them.

The existence of an all-powerful, personal God, I conclude, cannot be proved. At best what these arguments can do is reinforce already existing belief that God exists; they cannot persuade an unbeliever or sceptic that he does. But if all they can do is convince those that are already convinced, then they are utterly useless. Even more interestingly perhaps, they are paradoxical. What is really required of them, namely the ability to convince the sceptic, they cannot do; what they can do, on the other hand, is not worth doing. It cannot fail to be of interest here that Anselm's ontological argument, and by implication the other arguments, are designed to convince 'the fool' who has not already seen that God exists; for the believers they are quite simply redundant. Descartes too took a somewhat similar line, and prefaced his arguments by an apology to ecclesiastical authority for undertaking the task at all: it was not, he claimed, that God's existence really needed proof; but just in case there were faint-hearts or waverers, the arguments could come in handy. Some of the suspected motives behind Descartes's line of reasoning do not exactly show him as the most courageous of intellects, at least in relation to the Church. But that may be beside the point: there is no doubt that he regarded these proofs as being quite unnecessary for believers. What remains to be added is that they are also unconvincing to the unbeliever.

The demonstration of the existence of God, however, is not the only thing that is impossible: it is equally impossible to demonstrate God's non-existence. At a later stage, the real reason for both these impossibilities may become evident. For the time being, however, it may be desirable to discuss, in not-too-great detail, Findlay's demonstration of the non-existence of God,[7] which, to the best of my knowledge, is the only one if its kind; and fairness, if nothing else, demands that some notice be taken here of his attempt. The outline of his task is fairly simple. 'For we shall try to show', he says, 'that the Divine Existence can only be conceived in a religiously satisfactory manner, if we also conceive it as something inescapable and necessary, whether for thought or reality. From which it follows that our modern denial of necessity or rational evidence for such an existence amounts to a demonstration that there cannot be a God.' Findlay regards God 'as the adequate object of religious attitudes'; and defines religious attitude as 'one in which we tend to abase ourselves before some object, to defer to it wholly, to devote ourselves to it with unquestioning enthusiasm, to bend the knee before it, whether literally or metaphorically'. Now such an attitude, according to Findlay, would be justified or rational, as against insane, only if it happens to be the response to an object which is wholly appropriate, i.e. fully deserving of this attitude. Such an appropriate object would naturally have to be 'superior', in some sense; and by gradual refinement, this notion of superiority would take us to the theologian's idea of 'unlimited' or 'necessary being'; a being who does not just happen to exist, but cannot not exist; a being in whom essence and existence 'lose their separateness'. Such a being must also be one who possesses all his attributes in some necessary manner, and not simply contingently. Now, the proposition 'God is a necessary being' (in the two senses of necessity spoken of above) would be regarded by 'modern minds' as necessary only if it were either a tautology or else made necessary by the very use of words, 'the arbitrary conventions of language'. 'On such a view the Divine Existence could only be a necessary matter if we had made up our minds to speak theistically *whatever the empirical circumstances might turn out to be.*' This leads Findlay to conclude that the 'religious frame of mind' wishes to eat the cake and have it as well: 'It desires the Divine Existence both to have that inescapable character which can, in modern views, only be found where truth reflects an arbitrary convention, and also the character of "making a real difference", which is only possible where truth doesn't have this merely linguistic basis.' This, according to Findlay, must surely provide a *reductio ad absurdum* proof of God's non-existence.

Much can be said against Findlay's purported demonstration, but its main fault, as correctly pointed out by Hughes,[8] is that it assumes that if God's existence is necessary, it must be seen or known to be so. But this has not been established by Findlay and it is not easy to see how it can be. Yet it needs to be, since theologians who ascribe necessary existence to God take the view that 'God necessarily exists', while self-evident in itself, need not be so either to certain actual human beings, modern or otherwise, or even to human reason at its best. Aquinas in particular denies that 'God exists' is necessary in the last of the senses, namely, that it will be evident even to human reason at its best. Hence God's necessary being would seem to be quite compatible with 'our modern denial of necessity or rational evidence for such an existence'. Findlay's minor premise, therefore, fails to do what it is required to, i.e. the denial of the consequent in his hypothetical major premise; and hence the demonstration fails. Hughes makes certain other perceptive criticisms too, but the one just outlined is the main one, and I want to leave it at that, except to point out one thing.

Findlay's analysis of God 'as the adequate object of religious attitudes' and his observation that this attitude 'was one in which we tended to abase ourselves . . .' etc, while helpful, does not, to my mind, succeed in uniquely identifying God as the object of such an attitude. There are plenty of examples in history of far less than divine beings eliciting such an attitude from their followers or admirers. On hindsight, or from a distance, such followers may well be characterised as insane rather than religious. But the difference evidently will not lie in the attitude, but something else. This point may be only incidental to the success or failure of his demonstration, but I think it is an important one none the less, for it should forewarn us that an adequate account of religion cannot be based on the explication of the religious attitude alone.

What must finally be said about it is that Findlay's ontological disproof of God's existence is just as misguided as the more traditional 'ontological proof'. For both commit the same sort of mistake, namely, the attempt to demonstrate the existence or non-existence of an entity from the mere concept of it. But if the existence of God cannot be so deduced, nor can his non-existence, except by showing the concept to be self-contradictory. If the proof seems to sound like a conjuror's act of producing something from a hat containing nothing, then the disproof must count as an instance of 'dematerialisation' of something that might be in existence, both absurd by normal criteria of judgment.

The other familiar way in which, indirectly at least, the 'demonstration' of God's non-existence has been attempted is by showing the utter incoherence of the concept. If the concept, it is argued implicitly, cannot mean anything, then there is nothing to which it could refer either. One of the best known examples of this approach is Flew's where he contends that claims about God's existence (and other such theological utterances), if treated as making sense, meet 'death by a thousand qualifications'.[9] This is not strictly an attempted disproof of God's existence, but an argument designed to show that all theological utterances (including the one asserting God's existence) are either false or nonsensical, because they are untestable.

It cannot, however, fail to be of interest here that, according to Nielsen, 'Much contemporary analytical work in the philosophy of religion has abandoned any attempt to find a general meaning criterion in virtue of which the putative truth-claims of religion can be shown to be unintelligible or incoherent and has gone instead into the detail of actual theological argument in an attempt to establish the actual incoherence or at least the baselessness of religious and theological claims.'[10] And, as he rightly points out, this is true of Flew too, as, for example, in his *God and Philosophy*. This is an interesting development for our present purposes. 'God exists' may still be claimed to be incoherent, but since the claim would be based not on any general grounds of meaning or methodology but on the merits of the particular proposition, it is in principle possible to dispute the claim, thus rendering the issue of God's existence at least debatable. An excellent example of this is the attempt by Richard Swinburne to establish the coherence of theism.[11]

As far as I am aware, the only other attempt even vaguely resembling a demonstration of God's non-existence is Paul Ziff's.[12] While I disagree with certain details of his argument, I have some sympathy with his very guarded conclusion that there is good reason to suppose that the existence of a being answering to 'the plain man's conception of God' is incompatible with modern physical theory. This is not surprising: modern *physical* theory would be hardly so if it accommodated the existence of a supposedly 'spiritual' entity. Also it is not self-evident that the plain man's conception of God is what Ziff thinks it is, irrespective of cultural contexts. But above all, it is clear that Ziff's argument is far from any demonstration of God's non-existence, for the admission of incompatibility between modern physical theory and God's existence does not by itself entail that it is the latter that must be rejected. Ziff himself says, 'present physical theory, however, does not suffice to establish the non-existence of God; at best, it suffices to establish the non-existence of God as now conceived of by a plain man'.[13] In the light of remarks I have just made, one may wonder if it does even that.

What is most important to note, however, is that even if the demonstration of the non-existence of a personal God were possible, it would not in the least show that religion itself was impossible or that religious belief was a form of self-deception. It will only show that belief in such a God was a delusion. For it is entirely possible to have a religion without God. It is this that makes the attempted demonstration of God's existence or non-existence so pointless; and also provides the most telling argument against theocentrism. What made it so important for the believer to demonstrate that God exists and for the sceptic to establish that he does not, was the assumption that there could be no religion without God. But we know that there are religions without the concept of one supreme, personal God. I am well aware that Ninian Smart, Peter Winch and Konstantin Kolenda, among others, have, from somewhat different perspectives, stressed the possibility of religion without God. But I am not convinced that the point has been grasped firmly or widely enough, and hence still needs to be made continually, if only to offset the continued hold of the contrary impression.

The recognition of polytheism as a religion entails that belief in one, personal God is not necessary for the concept of religion; and we know that the religion of many peoples in the past was polytheistic, e.g. the Greeks, the Romans and the Indians. Indeed in India polytheism, it could be said, survives alongside other forms of belief; and the belief-systems of many tribes and peoples in the world today are polytheistic. Sometimes, one reads accounts of ancient cultures, e.g. the Maoris of New Zealand or the Kulin of Australia, where it appears that their polytheistic faith did, after all, contain a sort of 'father figure' or 'high god' resembling the Western notion of God in some respects.[14] But it is not always clear, not to me at any rate, whether this was not the result of the European narrator's tendency to superimpose his own familiar concepts onto these foreign but ancient cultures.

Besides, there are religions (at least religious schools) for whom God, or rather its equivalent, is impersonal, e.g. the Advaita Vedānta school of Hinduism and certain forms of mysticism. Advaita Vedānta does postulate a universal consciousness, *Brahman*, as the ground of the universe, but insists that it is impersonal. Even more importantly, there are religious systems with no God at all, e.g. early Buddhism and its present Theravāda school, and the Mīmāmsā and Sāmkhya schools of Hinduism. It is not possible to dismiss these schools as non-religion, for Hinduism itself has regarded them as atheistic but otherwise well within its main body. Indeed, Mīmāmsā has often been regarded, justly I think, as the bastion of Hindu orthodoxy, just as Advaita Vedānta has often been called the 'crown' of Hinduism. In any case, there can be no dispute that early Buddhism and Theravāda, as indeed Jainism, do not provide for a God: the reverential or worshipful attitudes to the Buddha and to Mahavira, respectively, are due solely to their being enlightened teachers and founders of the faiths. In the past, sometimes European scholars, starting from their understandable but wrong assumption that the Judaeo-Christian form was the paradigm of religion 'proper', tended to treat these other faiths as somehow 'deviant'. How else can one explain the question 'Is Buddhism a religion?', discussed seriously in a textbook on philosophy of religion that I remember reading as an undergraduate in India? It seems that unless one is determined to give a highly prescriptive account, these other forms of belief would have to be regarded as genuine specimens of religion.

The conclusion seems unavoidable that from the point of view of the definition of religion, the highly specific concept of a supreme, personal God is not required. The belief in a personal God, or his existence, is not a necessary condition of religion: the concept ought to be explicable without this notion. It is possible to argue that belief in God is not a sufficient condition of religion either. For one can imagine an individual or a whole community who believe in God but still live such atrocious lives that one would have the greatest compunction in ascribing the name of religion to their way of life. Equally, if this individual or community merely gave a kind of intellectual assent to God's existence, but did not let this belief reflect itself in appropriate attitudes and actions, then, I suspect, it would be hard to regard it as religious. But this is, strictly speaking, beside the point for our present purposes, which is to delineate what may or may not be essential to the concept of religion. The point of my argument should not be misconstrued as implying that God's existence or non-existence does not matter: to those who believe, it is what matters most; and to those determined to remain unbelievers too it matters a great deal, for if God could somehow be shown to exist, only the insane would remain unbelievers. My point simply is that a definition of religion, if it is not to be overtly prejudicial to its non-theistic forms, must be formulated in such a way that it does not specifically incorporate any reference to God. On the other hand, it must not be couched in terms which tend to exclude theistic forms; for, while the concept of God may not be integral to all religions, there is not the slightest doubt that it is so to some of the most important ones. There can be religion, either with or without the concept of God.

# 3 Towards a Definition

Our discussion so far has been directed towards the formulation of some of the desiderata that, I believe, are relevant to the definition of religion. A truly satisfactory account of religion must satisfy many other conditions, of course; but the need to ensure that it is truly descriptive and universal in scope, is not excessively theocentric, nor reductionist, and that it accommodates non-institutionalised and personal expressions of religiosity, would seem to be fairly basic.

Throughout the first two chapters and in the course of what I have just said above I may be considered guilty of having made a questionable assumption, namely, the desirability, even the possibility, of defining 'religion' adequately. Why assume, it may be asked, that the many and varied phenomena we characterise as religions or religious sects have some unique and unvarying set of properties in common? Why not face the 'fact' that Hinduism, Islam, Christianity, Zen Buddhism and Taoism, the magico-religious practices of the Azande, and the Trobriand Indians, the tribal religions of Africa and of the aborigines of Australia, in so far as they are all religions, merely display what Wittgenstein called 'family resemblances'? There is, I must confess, a great deal of force in this suggestion, deriving not merely from the authority of Wittgenstein. But I have my reasons – good ones, I hope – for not letting it be the last word. For a start, it is my firm belief that, despite the wide variations in doctrine and practice, there are certain features that all these religions do seem to share. Moreover, even accepting the idea that there are no more than 'family resemblances' among the many examples of religion, it does not seem to me altogether pointless to ask what it is in respect of which the family resemblance may appropriately be said to hold. It may be that my actual effort to pinpoint these features will prove abortive, but, in view of my belief to the contrary, it would be wrong to assume failure at the outset. On the other hand, if I were to succeed in providing a minimal definition of some sort, even if only a 'loose thread', as it were, it could prove useful in the task of the identification and discussion of concepts and problems in religion requiring philosophical investigation.

What I must state emphatically is that my attempt is not intended to be a search for some hidden essence whose presence or absence could automatically determine whether something was or was not to count as religion. I am under no illusion whatsoever that such a 'hard' definition could be found: my acceptance of the notion of family resemblance among religions would seem to imply that the features in respect of which they show this resemblance can only be characterised in very broad, possibly tentative, terms. As I have stated repeatedly, my aim is to give a descriptive, rather than a prescriptive or stipulative, account of religion. This means that it will always be open to a critic to come up with an example of what is actually recognised as religion but which does not satisfy one or another of the 'requirements' of my definition, and thus challenge its adequacy or correctness. I am trying to explicate a concept in use, rather than attempting to legislate how it ought to be used. I am fully mindful, too, that 'religion' is an empirical concept; and, as Waismann pointed out, all empirical concepts have an 'open texture'.[1] That is to say 'that we can never exclude altogether the possibility of some unforeseen situation arising in which we shall have to modify our definition'.[2] With these provisos, however, I feel it is time to move towards the actual task of definition itself.

The starting-point for such an enterprise has in the end to be arbitrary; for as long as the end-product, i.e. the definition, in this case, is adequate, it does not matter how it was arrived at. I wish to start by noting that all religions and religious sects, recognised as such, seem to refer to or presuppose one or more entities, states or processes which are said to lie 'beyond experience', i.e. ordinary experience. In the case of theistic faiths, the most notable among such 'transcendental' entities is, of course, God, as exemplified paradigmatically by the Judaeo-Christian tradition, including Islam. Even in these religions, however, God is not the only transcendental item: references to heaven and hell, the day of judgment, and the like, also occur. Among examples of religion discussed earlier as being those that do not postulate a supreme, personal God, we find that they nevertheless incorporate belief in certain other entities, states, etc that can only be described as transcendental. Advaita Vedānta, for example, postulates *Brahman*; and Buddhism and Jainism speak of *Nirvāna* (or its equivalent). The Mīmāmsā doctrine postulates *Apūrva* or *Adrista*, literally meaning 'the unseen', which 'organises' the affairs of the world, including the moral deserts of human action; and the Sāmkhya asserts the evolution of the world from a primordial stuff, called *Prakriti*. Polytheistic religions, apart from ascribing supernatural attributes to their gods and goddesses, invariably also have a 'place' or sphere (in some sense) beyond this world, which happens to be the abode of gods and goddesses and of humans who eventually get elevated to those ranks. To my knowledge, there is no religion which does not speak of one or more of such 'unseen' agencies, states, etc. Humanism, and even less plausibly, Marxism, could be cited as exceptions, but the former, whatever the occasional appearance, was introduced by its pioneers as an alternative to religion; and I cannot think of a sensible humanist today who is likely to be offended if what he stands for is excluded from the list of religions. In the case of Marxism, it seems to me that its occasional description as religion cannot be any more than an euphemism, highlighting the intensity of belief of some Marxists, which has normally been associated with religion.

In saying this, however, I have no wish to dismiss quickly the claims of humanism and Marxism, to be religions, just in order to make my definition look more plausible. Perhaps a case can be made for the recognition of either or both as religion,[3] by arguing either that they do in fact invoke principles which could be said to be transcendental or by suggesting that there are, otherwise, good grounds for treating them as religion, although they do not appeal to any transcendental items. The former line of argument, if sound, would in fact reinforce my own claim, namely, that there is no religion without some 'transcendental' agencies, powers, principles etc. But what if the second line of argument succeeds? Would that necessarily destroy the very basis of my definition? In the unlikely event of that hypothetical situation actually obtaining, there would obviously be a case for modifying the definition which I am approaching. But it would seem to be unnecessary to provide for that eventuality now. Since the concept of religion has an 'open texture', a *complete definition*, i.e. ' a thought-model which anticipates and settles for all every possible question of usage',[4] would be out of the question here, as in the case of any other empirical concept. But, then, such a complete definition is far from what I am seeking anyway: I am merely trying to delineate certain features that could be said to characterise what are now unquestionably recognised as religions.

If what I have just argued is correct, then, I believe, it helps us to identify one universal feature shared by all religions; and might thus give us a starting-point for a definition. The problem, however, is that all these terms avowedly refer to transcendental items and it could be, and is,[5] argued that they present serious philosophical problems, even 'logical muddles', regarding their coherence or intelligibility; and hence, the argument might run, a definition based on this 'discovery' can hardly lead to any philosophical illumination. Whether there is anything in this opinion can only be discussed in any detail at a later stage. For the moment, I only intend to mention two relevant facts. The first is that we set out to provide a descriptive account of religion, and any suggestion that terms and concepts crucial to it could be dismissed at the outset and without careful examination, as non-significant or muddled, would be rendering ourselves guilty of passing a value judgment on religion in general, and thus of acting contrary to our professed aim. Judgment on this and similar issues is not precluded, provided there is a suitable context. But at the moment, we must simply note whatever features promise to be universal, in order to see if they can provide us with any common and more or less essential properties of religion. Moreover, it is plain that these concepts are intelligible to vast numbers of people who practise these religions and there are sizeable cultures and communities successfully communicating through their use. Given this, it would be methodologically wrong to assume otherwise, especially since our avowed task is descriptive; although this does not entail that if one or more of them turns out in the course of fuller investigation to be lacking in significance, according to well spelt-out criteria, there would be any reason to refrain from saying so. At this stage, however, fairness would seem to demand that these entities, states, processes, etc, be regarded as intelligible but non-empirical, that is to say, *theoretical*. Most higher level scientific theories postulate items which, while required by the theory, are not open to direct observation or experiment and are, in this sense, non-empirical.

Characterising them as theoretical, however, is not enough. Some further specification is required in order to show whether and, if so, how they are different, for instance, from scientific theoretical entities. It seems that a good way of demarcating the former might be to call them *metaphysical*. These entities, etc are not only non-empirical, in the sense of being incapable of observation and experiment, at a given time, but also 'non-scientific'. For they seem to be embedded in explanatory theories about the world as a whole: some at least of the statements of religion seem to me to be designed to express what the world is like, and why, according to the religion in question. This claim, as indeed certain others made above, will require elaboration and justification later, which I undertake in chapter 4. What needs to be noted now is that theories purporting to explain the nature and significance of the world as a whole (as against scientific ones which only describe specific aspects of it) are typically regarded as philosophical or, more specifically, metaphysical (in the traditional, non-pejorative sense of 'metaphysics'). As I hope to show later, there is no reason why a once-metaphysical entity cannot eventually become a *scientific*-theoretical one. This has, indeed, often happend in the history of science: 'atom', 'gravity', 'force' and the like, may be just some examples of metaphysical-theoretical entities subsequently turning into scientific ones. At any rate, we may now be in a position to say that a proposition is metaphysical only if it (or the sentence expressing it) refers to or presupposes one or more of the kinds of entities (states, etc) characterised earlier as metaphysical-theoretical. It would seem to follow from my account so far that a system of belief cannot normally be considered religious unless at least some of its propositions are metaphysical, in the sense suggested above. In other words, it would seem to be a necessary condition for a belief-system to be religious that some at least of its propositions be metaphysical. It is my contention that these metaphysical propositions are absolutely central to a religion in as much as all its other propositions depend on or presuppose them, in some measure. In view of this, the former may be called primary and the latter secondary or derivative. What should perhaps be added is that if my account of religion seems to put an excessive stress on metaphysical propositions, it is because these are regarded as primary, and not because there are not any others.

As hinted earlier, I agree with those who take the view that religious systems are, partly at least, explanatory theories, although a defence of this view must await a subsequent occasion. But it seems to me that what such theories seek to explain is not, typically, the world revealed in ordinary experience, nor, obviously, the one postulated in scientific theory; but rather an uncommon 'perception', or experience of the world or of its significance, usually enjoyed (or suffered?) by the proponent of a religion. Such uncommon perceptions, experiences, or intuitions are individual and highly personal. Certainly, the intensity of these experiences may be unique to the founders of the religions concerned. It seems obvious that unless a certain way of looking at, or responding to, the world was felt by the founder to be deeply moving and full of significance, the phenomenal events that the beginnings of some of these religions undoubtedly have been, would not have taken place. Nevertheless, such experiences must, in my opinion, be held to be in principle repeatable, i.e. others may, under certain circumstances, have the same[6] or similar perceptions, too. This as I will argue later, may account for the continuing appeal and vitality of a given religion.

It is possible to say that what I have called 'highly personal uncommon experiences or perceptions' are rather like Hare's 'bliks', strong but, in some sense, 'insane' dispositions to view the world, or certain features of it, in specific, perhaps peculiar, ways.[7] If we choose to draw this parallel, however, we must be careful to bear in mind that every 'blik', every disposition to view the world in a certain way, need not be the outcome of personal *experience* in the sense of an identifiable psychological event. It may, on the contrary, be the result of a hunch, of philosophical speculation, of an arbitrary act of decision, or simply of an eccentric streak in one's personality. What is important is that whichever way they arise, once they have arisen, they function in the same way as powerful and deeply moving personal experiences do: they do not leave everything as it was; the perception of the world is transformed, 'coloured', imbued with new significance. The natural world acquires non-natural meanings. And it is questions regarding the why and wherefore of this transformed world that lead to the explanatory metaphysical theory. It should be clear, then, that unlike Hare, I do not regard these 'bliks' as 'insane', and hence, unexplained and inexplicable terminal points in one's world-view; they are merely the data of experience requiring explanation.

One or two cautionary remarks may be called for here. The suggested separation of theory from experience and their order of precedence is not meant to be of a chronological, but rather, of a logical nature. If this is not realised, serious difficulties in my explication may be seen to arise. For there are religions which have no historical founders and where we know very little about their historical origins. In these cases we cannot justifiably talk of a temporal sequence of experiences or 'bliks' and a theory following these. The literature, and other records, of these religions reveal evidence of the relevant theory and practices and of the unusual perception or 'bliks' together, in one body, making judgments about any temporal order extremely hazardous, if not impossible. Apart from this practical difficulty in the determination of the actual sequence, if any, however, we need also to note the fact that nothing may be lost by reversing the order. It is entirely possible that in one or another case the theory and the experience were 'revealed' simultaneously, or that the theory itself somehow arose first, thus providing the conceptual framework for subsequent experiences of the relevant sort. For philosophical purposes the chronology is irrelevant anyway. But since the experience or 'bliks', on the one hand, and the theory, on the other, can be distinguished; and since in the case of at least some religions there seems to be evidence for supposing that certain experiences by the founders preceded the theory, we will speak (admittedly with inadequate historical backing) *as if* this sequence was characteristic of all religions. That brings me to the mention of another 'as if'. In the case of those religions that do allow us to speak of certain psychological experiences of an unusual kind and intensity preceding the articulation of the relevant belief-systems, there usually seems to be some evidence of a period of reflection or speculation following the initial experience, as will be discussed later. It may not, therefore, be altogether inappropriate to speak as if the theory arises in deliberate speculation, contemplation, or 'conjecture', undertaken to seek an explanation of the experiences or 'bliks'. This mode of speaking is adopted without prejudice to the claims of certain religions that the 'truths' preached by them had been 'revealed' to their founders, prophets or wise men. While these claims have to be recorded, their truth cannot be accepted or rejected on any *a priori* grounds that I am aware of. Consequently, even if some of them were, or turned out to be, true on proper assessment, their epistemological status, initially, has to be that of 'conjectures' or hypotheses requiring verification or falsification, although this is not how practitioners of the relevant religions will view them. With all this clarification, however, perhaps it is time to illustrate the suggested outline with the actual example of a religion.

It seems to me that 'the four noble truths' of Buddhism exemplify quite clearly this movement from initial 'bliks' to full, explanatory metaphysical theories about them. The unusual perception in this case is expressed by the first noble truth, i.e. that 'there is suffering', which, as is well known, is taken to mean that the whole process of being – birth, illness, decay and death – is characterised by suffering. The story of the Buddha's anguish, caused by his intense perception of suffering in the world, and his subsequent renunciation of his kingdom and family in search for a way out of it, is very familiar. Not every person encountering the facts of birth, sickness, old age and death is gripped, in the way the Buddha was, by the overpowering awareness that life itself was suffering and that something must be done about it. The experience is uncommon, very personal and exceedingly intense, leading to his long and arduous experimentation with many possible paths said to result in release from suffering, and culminating in the formulation of his 'eightfold path'. Anyway, the second noble truth postulates 'ignorance' (*Avidyā*) – mediated by twelve links – as the cause of suffering; and since it is assumed that everything must have a cause, and also that whatever is caused can be destroyed by removing or undoing the cause, the third noble truth affirms the possibility of the cessation of pain. Finally, the fourth one discloses the way that leads to the cessation of suffering, i.e. the eightfold path. In this transition from the first to the fourth noble truth, many metaphysical entities and processes are postulated until the explanation is deemed to be complete. It is true that the schematic way in which Buddhist teachings, especially the four noble truths, are set out lends particular plausibility to my claims; but it is my belief that most religions will support the pattern I outlined of initial 'bliks', followed, or accompanied, by an explanatory metaphysical theory.

What I have said so far has, however, given us no basis to distinguish religious from other metaphysical theories. We cannot yet explain why Hegelianism and even Platonism are not, while Buddhism and, say, Mormonism, are, readily regarded as religions, when in fact all of these are belief-systems containing at least some metaphysical propositions, in the sense outlined above. To some extent, the difference between religion and other kinds of metaphysical systems may be said to lie in the nature and details of the metaphysics, but in the main, I think, it would seem to be in what is done with it, or, what commonly accompanies it. In my opinion, what sets religious metaphysical doctrines apart is that they somehow succeed in eliciting or evoking deep, personal *commitment* on the part of individuals who usually get recognised as members of distinct communities. It may be tempting to argue that there must be something intrinsic to the quality of a particular metaphysics if it is to produce this commitment; and in some instances it may be possible to substantiate this claim, to an extent, anyway. But careful reflection will be unlikely to sustain it. The commitment has, on the whole, to be explained in terms of historical, psychological or other socio-empirical factors, and not any logical features of the metaphysics in question. In a moment I shall endeavour to say a bit more about the nature of this commitment, but it seems to me that, in the context of definition, the main ingredients of religion are experience (including 'bliks'), metaphysics and commitment. Matthew Arnold characterised religion as 'ethics heightened . . . by feeling'. In the light of my analysis so far, however, but, of course, bearing in mind the hazards of over-simplification inevitably involved in attempting short, easily mouthable, definitions of complex phenomena, it would seem preferable to call religion 'metaphysics enlivened by experience and personal commitment'.

Speaking purely factually, this commitment would seem to be on three distinct, though clearly related, levels. I would call them (a) *belief*-commitments, (b) *attitude*-commitments, and (c) *action*-commitments. When a person commits himself to a religion, he accepts that the metaphysical entities, etc. postulated by the relevant system do actually exist. He does not, for example, consider them merely logically possible or philosophically plausible. He *assumes* the truth of the metaphysical propositions asserted or implied by the religion in question, as indeed of certain other propositions. For the believer, that is, they are not tentative hypotheses awaiting verification or falsification by events, or even philosophical examination by rational criteria. A believer, in the very act of adopting a religion, especially when this is the result of a conscious choice, accepts a certain ontology, although, as I will argue later, this acceptance is not as irrevocable nor as immune to criticism as certain philosophers would have us believe. The details of what precise items constitute his ontology will naturally vary according to the choice of religion, but every religious person, it would appear, does accept the existence of certain metaphysical entities, e.g. God, soul, immortality, heaven, reincarnation, redemption, liberation and the like. It is this feature that I have called 'belief-commitments'.

What I have chosen to describe as 'attitude-commitments' may, in a sense, be said to follow from belief-commitments. But whether they strictly do so or not, it is clear that a believer's beliefs are accompanied by certain attitudes considered appropriate to the objects of his belief, so considered by the religion that happens to be his, not another. For instance, a Christian will not only take it for granted that God exists. He must also be obliged to regard God as mighty and just and worthy only of our filial love. A Hindu's disposition to treat God as someone familiar and, therefore, as the object also of more mundane kinds of love, e.g. that between husband and wife or brother and sister, will be deemed highly improper if entertained by a Christian. Similarly, certain objects or events – in the widest sense of the words – must be regarded as sacred, e.g. the Cross or the Eucharist for the Christian; the cow or the *Agnihotra* ceremony for the Hindu; the *Dhamma* and the *Sangha* for the Buddhist; the Talmud and the Passover for the Jew, to name only a few. Among attitude-commitments, special mention must be made of those which, while more abstract in nature and, therefore, possibly liable to interpretation and reinterpretation, are none the less the most profound ones, not least because they have the most important social implications. Examples of such attitudes are those relating to other people, to other forms of life, to situations of stress in life, to the facts of life and death themselves. The attitude enjoined by Christianity, for instance, is supposed to be one of brotherly love to other people, though when it comes to other creatures, it is only so, if it is, on special interpretation. For the Buddhist, and more notably the Jaina, on the other hand, it is one of reverence for all life, with the Hindu perhaps coming in between the Christian on the one hand and the Buddhist and the Jaina on the other. Attitudes of the kind of which the above is only one example include such intangible but important ones as those relating to man's place in the universe and, therefore, to the resources of nature. It should be evident that so-called attitude-commitments are often hard to separate from belief-commitments; and indeed it is possible, in principle, to render one of the former into one of the latter. But despite this point of principle, it is, in my opinion, desirable for the two sets of commitments to be distinguished, if only for the reason that belief-commitments by themselves will not adequately, perhaps not at all, account for the emotional tone surrounding religious beliefs and practices.

Finally, religious belief, perhaps more so than certain other beliefs of a purely factual kind, invariably issues forth in certain kinds of action or behaviour to which the believer feels obligated. Thus, while belief and attitude-commitments provide the cognitive and affective components of religion, action-commitments provide the conative element; and so together cover the whole spectrum of the complexity of religion, often aptly described as a complete 'way of life'. Behaviour and action of appropriate kinds, it will be realised, is not just incidental to religion, any more or less than the other two sorts of commitments mentioned earlier. In fact on certain views of religion, that we will have occasion to consider in detail later, this is the most essential factor; for, it can be argued, it is his actions and behaviour that ultimately provide a test of the sincerity or otherwise of the believer's professed beliefs. For example, if someone believes, in keeping with his faith, that there is life after death, he would be expected to show through his actions that he does not regard his present life as much more than a transitional phase, and that, therefore, he is not excessively preoccupied with the pleasures of this world in the way a hedonist would be. But if in all he does he gives evidence of acting in ways which betray his feeling of uncertainty or anxiety that this may be his last and only encounter with the world, then we may have good grounds for concluding that he only professes to but does not really believe in an after-life. Quite independently of whether or not actions provide evidence of genuineness of belief, however, and speaking purely descriptively, it seems that religion is invariably associated with practices of certain sorts. The range of such practices is found to vary among religions. Some religions enjoin (or are seen by the believer to do so) a great many injunctions and prohibitions, rituals and ceremonies, forms of prayer, worship and meditation, so as to cover almost all of an individual's waking life. The form of Hindusim often known as 'Brāhminism', Tibetan Buddhism, certain forms of Catholicism and Judaism may be said to be examples of such religion, as indeed may be certain tribal faiths and specimens of so-called 'primitive' religion. Others may content themselves with only a few general guidelines governing an individual's life-style, and mainly relating to a believer's moral and spiritual outlook. Perhaps Advaita Vedānta, early Buddhism and certain forms of Protestantism exemplify this.

In an earlier anticipation of the present analysis, I had named this set of commitments the 'moral' commitment.[8] But in view of the range of practices associated with religions, including prayer, worship, ritual, sacrifice, even magic, the use of the word 'moral' to designate them all is bound to be misleading. It is true that all religions tend to regulate, in varying degrees, behaviour which can properly be said to be the sphere of morality; but it is equally clear that these constitute only a small, though important, subset of the wide range of actions and behaviour with which religion seems to be concerned. In recognition of this fact, and with a view to using a term which is not obviously value-loaded, the phrase 'action-commitment' seems to me to be the better choice.

Perhaps there is more to the concept of religion than my present analysis has been able to capture. In relation to specific examples of religion, I suspect that this will almost certainly be the case. But in the context of a general definition, which is not prescriptive or reductionist, it seems to me that the only features which can be aptly considered common and, in some sense, essential to religion are these. Firstly, it seems to spring from or be charged by certain unusual experiences, perceptions, or 'bliks'. Secondly, these 'bliks' are followed or attended by a metaphysical theory; and, finally, such a theory is invariably attended by the three kinds of commitment mentioned above. Speaking somewhat more formally, perhaps the following definition may be suggested. A religion is a metaphysical theory rooted in experience and commanding deep, personal commitment to certain beliefs, attitudes and actions on the part of its follower(s), such commitment being (or being seen as) entailed by the theory in question. Further elaboration and defence of this account, as indeed the examination of what consequences its acceptance has for philosophy of religion, will be the task of subsequent chapters.

# 4 Religion and Religions

My intention in this chapter is to see to what extent, if any, my proposed definition satisfies the desiderata outlined earlier, and, if possible, to pinpoint certain implications of my account, which may either help subsequent discussion of philosophical issues, or for other reasons deserve mention but may not easily find a suitable context in the rest of the book. It seems to me that, whatever else may be said against it, the definition cannot be said to suffer from theocentrism: 'God' does not occur in it. On the other hand, though, those religions to which the concept of God is central, cannot be said to be excluded from the scope of the definition, for propositions about God will be straightforwardly seen as a subset of those constituting the metaphysical theory, which is, explicitly and importantly, a part of the definition offered. This seems to me so obvious that I will not argue it any further.

I cannot see that it is reductionist in any way, for all it does is identify features that seem commonly, or universally, to characterise religion. Since religions, whatever else they may be, are belief-systems based on certain unusual experiences or perceptions, it is important first to identify, and then to describe the nature of what it is that is believed. It is evident that it is only propositions that can be said to be believed, asserted, doubted or disputed. Further reflection makes it clear that these propositions can only be described as metaphysical, in the sense suggested in my analysis; and that such propositions are embedded as central statements occurring in the theory that describes the beliefs and claims of the religion in question. No attempt is made either to say or imply, at least not consciously, that religion is, or should be taken to be, something other than what it appears to be.

Is it prescriptive in any way? The first thing that must be said is that my intention has been to offer a purely descriptive account. But have I succeeded in carrying out my intention, or have I either unwittingly or deliberately allowed the definition to become prescriptive in some way after all? I cannot myself see that the latter has happened, though I must allow the logical possibility that this may indeed be the case. It is not too difficult to anticipate the charge that, having complained that prevailing accounts of religion did not, or did not sufficiently, pay regard to Eastern religions, I have, in my own account, overcompensated and gone to the other extreme: that my analysis does not accommodate, at least not very comfortably, non-Eastern religions. If true, this charge would be powerful enough to destroy any plausibility that my characterisation of religion may have. But I believe that it is false and, if and in so far as it is seriously entertained, must be based on a misunderstanding. I have admittedly illustrated my account with the help of an Eastern religion, Buddhism; but only because it seemed to me to be the religion that offers a particularly concise and clear example of what I was trying to say, and not because other religions cast doubt on it. On the contrary, the reason for suggesting this way of explicating the concept of religion was precisely my belief that it does justice to all religions. The soundness of my belief will, I hope, become apparent, if it is not already so, when we come to examine the scope of the suggested definition.

One other form in which I can see the accusation of 'prescriptivism' being made is the following. It may appear to some that in characterising the transcendental entities, etc. invoked by religion as metaphysical, I have, far from describing religion, relegated it to the class of nonsense. For have not many eminent philosophers since, and including, Hume declared all metaphysics to be only worthy of being consigned to the flames? In answer, it should be recalled that elsewhere I quite explicitly refrained from taking the view that metaphysical propositions are, as a matter of principle, all incoherent, though I allowed that specific examples of it may be. It follows then that though I have used the expression 'metaphysical', I have not intended to do so pejoratively or prescriptively. It just seemed to me that a theory containing propositions apparently referring to transcendental entities, etc could best be described as metaphysical; and in the previous chapter I gave my reasons why. I could, in fact, say that it was my desire to be scrupulously descriptive that forced upon me the choice of the word 'metaphysical'.

Isn't my definition, it may be asked, merely platitudinous? What it says about religion may be true, but perhaps so true as not to be worth mentioning. For all it seems to say is that religion consists of a theory which is metaphysical, which purports to be rooted in certain powerful experiences and which happens to draw personal commitment from believers. This impression is unavoidable, but it need not constitute a criticism. The definition of any concept must necessarily leave out characteristics that give flesh and bone to individuals designated by it. No individual human being we encounter can ever be adequately described as just a rational animal, unless these terms are seen as paraphrasing, through the use of concepts of wide scope, a host of properties that an actual human being has. Definition is not description, although a purported definition may be descriptive or prescriptive in character. If the definition offered is of a class, consisting of many individual members, then the terms occurring in it must of necessity be 'umbrella-words' capable of accommodating the many different forms in which a given property finds expression in particular members. The rationality of men is not expressed identically in all men nor is their animality. Likewise, the definition of religion cannot take account of specific experiences and metaphysical theories underlying the many religions nor can it properly name the belief, attitude, or action-commitments peculiar to any particular religion, far less of those of individual followers of the religion. All it can fairly be expected to do is to contain terms which do not exclude general properties that might be characteristic of any religion, especially what it shares with all the others. This, I believe, my definition does accomplish.

One way of vindicating the claim just made and of testing the adequacy of my account may be to show that it is capable of accommodating, under broad general terms, all or most of what W. P. Alston,[1] for example, calls 'religion-making characteristics'. I will discuss the nine listed by him with a view to assessing if these can be said to be covered by my definition. What I have to say in this connection applies, I believe, also to Smart's specification of the six 'dimensions' of religion[2] – the ritual, the mythological, the doctrinal, the ethical, the social and the experiential – although I do not directly discuss these. Alston's statement of the characteristic (or where necessary a brief paraphrase) is mentioned first, followed by my comments.

'Belief in supernatural beings (gods)(1).' It needs no arguing, I think, that this characteristic will be amply covered by that part of the definition which speaks of a 'metaphysical theory', especially in conjunction with the preceding relevant explanation. For 'supernatural beings', whether gods or demons, will be subsumed by 'transcendental entities, etc'.

'A distinction between sacred and profane objects (2),' and 'ritual acts focused on sacred objects (3)', will fall, though without being named, under what I have called 'attitude-commitments' and 'action-commitments', respectively. Characteristic (6) i.e. 'prayer and other forms of communication with gods', will seem adequately to come under 'action-commitments', in the broadest sense of 'action'. One qualification, however, is needed. Prayer, etc. need not, as I see it, be addressed to gods. In the more meditative, not to mention mystical, forms of religion, prayer is often indistinguishable from meditation; and so the object of prayer should not, in my opinion, be so narrowly specified.

Characteristic (4), listed by Alston, mentions 'a moral code believed to be sanctioned by the gods'. It seems to me that there are two important qualifications to be made here. A 'moral' code can only be incorporated as a characteristic of religion, if 'moral' is used up in a very loose sense, as signifying a code of injunctions and prohibitions which need not necessarily be of a 'moral' character, in the narrower sense of the word. For instance, orthodox Islamic convention enjoins prayer to be said five times every day, with the faithful facing towards Mecca. It is easily seen that, however important this may be as affirmation of one's Muslim faith, prayer is strictly speaking not an action that falls within the sphere of morality, at least of morality as usually discussed in philosophical textbooks on the subject. But, in the case of Islam in particular, praying is a very important social activity as well, which might be said to bring it fairly close to the sorts of duties falling under social obligation, and hence coming under the scope of morality. As Alston himself notes, in the narrower sense of morality, sacramental and mystical religions contain much that is amoral; for in the former sacrament, and in the latter experience of a certain kind, assume priority. Secondly, it should be clear in the light of remarks made earlier, and the definition, that the code need not be believed to be sanctioned 'by the gods'. This requirement would, again, make the definition rather narrow. In my opinion, it is enough for it to be *believed*, *somehow*, to be entailed by the metaphysical theory underlying the religion in question. With these provisos the substance of this particular characteristic is covered, I think, by 'action-commitments', together with the stipulation that these be seen by the believer to follow from the conjunction of primary and secondary propositions constituting the theory. The 'code', then, in so far as it would be regarded as consisting of a set of statements or commands of various sorts, would, on my analysis, constitute part of the total set of primary and derivative statements of the theory, or its implications. This fact, that the so-called moral code may largely be a subset of the derivative statement of the theory, is not accidental. In view of the point made earlier that sacramental and mystical religions in particular may contain much that is 'amoral', it would seem improper to incorporate the requirement of a moral code into the definition by its inclusion among the primary propositions of the theory, which are best described only as metaphysical. Moreover, the intended consequence of such a code, namely that believers see themselves as committed to specific sorts of action and behaviour, is quite clearly taken care of by the definition.

I now come to characteristics (5), (7) and (8). According to Alston, (5) consists of: 'Characteristically religious feelings (awe, sense of mystery, sense of guilt, adoration), which tend to be aroused in the presence of sacred objects and during the practice of ritual, and which are connected in idea with the gods.' This characteristic would seem to be well covered by that part of the definition which refers to experience, especially if this term is understood as including the two senses to be discussed later. Besides, in the somewhat brief discussion of attitude-commitments in the previous chapter it was pointed out that this particular set of commitments would embrace the 'feeling tone' of religion and consist largely of the kinds of feelings just described. Indeed, it is such feelings and attitudes, together with the firm, even passionate, commitment to act in certain ways that raises religious belief beyond mere intellectual assent.

Characteristic (7) stipulates 'a world view, or a general picture of the world as a whole and the place of the individual therein. This picture contains some specification of an overall purpose or point of the world and an indication of how the individual fits into it.' If it is recalled that, on my account, a metaphysical theory is part of the definition of religion, the requirement of a world view would seem to be well satisfied. As for the clause requiring, 'specification of an overall purpose or point of the world', it should be remembered that I regard the metaphysics forming the base of a religion as a theory designed to explain a highly personal, but possibly repeatable, experience or view of the world, the 'bliks', although not every religion may allow a clear separation of the experience from the theory. More often than not these 'bliks' will actually consist of a view of the point or purpose of the world: for example, Buddhism does not regard the world as the arena of pleasure or the abode of happiness, but as actually characterised by suffering from which, however, escape is possible. Finally, it will be recalled that I regard the experience and the theory, along with the three sets of commitments, to constitute a whole way of life, just what is required by Alston's characteristic (8). I will have something to say later regarding characteristic (9), i.e. 'a social group bound together' by the requirements of the other characteristics.

But it should be evident that I have much sympathy with Alston's analysis. I also take the spirit of his point that, instead of defining religion narrowly in terms of one or more of the above features, it is better to be flexible and recognise as a genuine instance of religion anything that satisfied a reasonable cluster of these characteristics. But, as explained in the previous chapter, I do believe that it is possible to organise the possible contents of these clusters around a 'loose thread', which is what my definition is meant to be. It should be clear that I do not share the view that a definition of 'cluster concepts' is altogether impossible.[3] Hence my specification of experience, the metaphysical theory and the three kinds of commitment as requirements for an adequate definition of religion which at the same time do not happen to be unduly restrictive, because of the wide scope of application of the terms employed.

Perhaps a word needs to be said about mystical, and other religious experience and how my account deals with it. This may be important, for it is often claimed that it is such experience that provides authenticity and the ultimate justification of religion. It is because in any religious tradition certain individuals have this experience, where they apparently come face to face with the divine or other metaphysical reality, that religion gets its continual rejuvenation and the affirmation of faith that is required from time to time. Indeed, since the nature of this reality is often held to be beyond intellectual apprehension, the articulation of this reality, however inadequately done, must, it is claimed, be ultimately based in such experience. Now, it will be recalled that, in my view, the metaphysical theory embedded in any religion is meant to explain the unusual perception or experience, usually relating to the point or purpose (or lack thereof) of the world. The incorporation of 'experience' into the definition is intended to take care of the possibility that the theory arises in and/or facilitates such experience, which may include the experience of God, of the 'holy', the 'numinous', or of the 'merger' of the self into the 'One', ground of the universe.

In the previous paragraph I have mainly examined whether my definition adequately provides for various kinds of religious experience, where experience can be understood primarily as a (set of) psychological event(s). But, as John Hick has pointed out, there is a different, although related, sense as well which needs to be recognised.[4] Drawing on a well-discussed recent philosophical distinction between 'seeing' and 'seeing-as', he suggests that faith ought to be understood also in terms of 'experiencing-as', i.e. the sense in which it provides the 'interpretative element within our cognitive religious experience'. For, as he says,

> there is a sense in which the religious man and the atheist both live in the same world and another sense in which they live consciously in different worlds. They inhabit the same physical environment and are confronted by the same changes occurring within it. But in its actual concrete character in their respective 'streams of consciousness' it has for each a different nature and quality, a different meaning and significance; for one does and the other does not experience life as a continual interaction with the transcendent God.[5]

Earlier in the same article, using Russell's distinction between knowledge by acquaintance and that by description, he talks of religious 'cognition in presence' (or by acquaintance) and 'cognition in absence' (or 'holding beliefs about'), and seems to be surprised that while biblical religious literature itself 'confidently presupposes a cognition of God by acquaintance, [our] theological literature in contrast recognises for the most part only cognition in absence'. Having noted these useful distinctions, it seems to me that my account adequately provides for experience in both relevant senses. When the context in which I introduced the term (deeply moving) 'experience' (perception, 'blik', etc.) is recalled, it should be evident that its occurrence in the definition is primarily designed to take account of 'cognition by acquaintance'. But when this is taken in conjunction with my point about the repeatability, in principle, of such experience, it will, I hope, be seen that it thus accommodates also what Hick calls 'experiencing-as'. Moreover, it must be borne in mind that the metaphysical *theory* required by the definition, together with the background of the synoptic 'vision' of the world recurring within a given tradition, will function as the paradigm or conceptual framework within which a religious person will perceive or interpret 'facts' about the world. The natural world, whatever that might be, will, by the believer, be experienced as having non-natural or extra-natural dimensions of meaning and value. The subjective experience(s) of the founder(s) of a religion may well account for the origins of the religion in question, but once it has come into being, it starts to function as the 'pigeon-holes' of perception by followers of the religion. The phrase relating to experience, in my definition, is intended to cover both senses of the term.

It may be objected that in defining it as a *deep*, personal commitment, I have taken a somewhat 'elitist' view of religion. For, it may be said, there are numerous followers of any religion whose faith is neither noticeably personal nor particularly deep. To them religion is meaningful only in so far as it is a social activity, not commanding any great sacrifices, except from fear of communal disapproval or other sanctions. We will shortly be examining this communal aspect of religion. As for the depth of commitment, it seems to me that without it neither the origin nor the continuing development of religion can be possible; nor would it be distinguishable from mere intellectual assent. It is this depth of commitment that allows the belief to issue, through the appropriate attitudes, into religious activity in the form of ritual, ceremonial and moral practices. The followers of a religion whose depth of commitment is questionable, are, it is fair to say, not the best of its exemplars; and the concept of religion should not be modelled after them.

While talking about the uncommon perception, or 'blik', that gives rise to a religion, I suggested that this was personal, but repeatable. This repeatability, it seems to me, is a factor in the growth of religious communities. Whether arising spontaneously or as a result of the success of the founder in evoking in his followers a perception similar to his own, it is this fact of shared or sharable perceptions that gives rise to a community of individuals with similar or identical beliefs. Again, it is because of this repeatability that it becomes possible for succeeding generations, through, of course, the experience of rare individuals, to reassert the 'truth' of their faith. This is not to say that but for this factor there might not be a community at all: the common human failing of uncritical regard for authority, the power of charismatic figures, not to mention simple human gullibility, could together ensure the rise of a community. But it seems to me that without this renewed experience of the original perception at least by some individuals from time to time, the religion in question would quickly degenerate into a mechanical congregation of individuals and cease to be the vital, dynamic community that the best of them usually are. Be that as it may, the point I now want to make is this. The community of believers is a historical or sociological fact about religion, and a very important one too. But in my opinion, this is not required for the explication of the concept itself, except in the context of a sociology of religion. A sociologist giving an account of religion must, almost by definition, pay primary regard to its communal or social aspects. A philosopher of religion, however, is only concerned with the logical features of the beliefs, attitudes and practices, etc. recognised as this or that religion. This means that philosophically speaking, it is not wrong to see religion simply as the experiences, beliefs and personal commitments of an individual, although this is not to say that where a society or community is actually there, the social focus of the beliefs and commitments could, or should, be ignored. The philosophical concept of religion, therefore, is quite hospitable to what I had called non-institutionalised, personal forms of religion: there is no reason why a particular religion cannot have just one follower, although in practice this is not often the case. The absence of a community should not count against something being a religion. It is evident, then, that Smart's 'social dimension' of religion and Alston's characteristic (9), namely, 'a social group bound together' by the requirements of the other eight characteristics,[6] is not, in my opinion, a necessary constituent of the concept of religion, but only a contingent fact important for the history and sociology of religion.

I must advise a certain amount of caution in construing this point, for misunderstandings are, otherwise, very likely. I am not in the least advocating that the social aspects of religion, where these are relevant or important, be disregarded: merely that religion should not be defined in such a way that a religion without a community becomes a conceptual impossibility or the attempt to say that there is one is deemed a linguistic impropriety. My reason for saying this is not just that one can easily think of a hypothetical individual whom one would unhesitatingly want to call religious but who is not recognisably a member of a community with shared beliefs and practices. More importantly, I think that a failure to recognise this may raise tricky questions, such as 'Was the Buddha a Buddhist?', or 'Was Mohammed a Mohammedan?' It is true that the former was born a Hindu, but in very important respects he was not a Hindu. If he had been, his teachings would not have been seen as the beginnings of a new religion. Yet the community of Buddhists came into being precisely because there was a powerful, 'enlightened' being who was already preaching and practising a new way of life. What shall we say of the Buddha in the interregnum? Did he have a religion, or did he not? To say that he did not, would seem to be odd, to put it mildly. On the other hand, to say that he did becomes problematic if we insist that religion must presuppose a community. I am not suggesting that it is, in any important sense, necessary to be able to put a name to the Buddha's faith. On the contrary, I am saying that quite independently of the community of Hindus, against whose faith he had rebelled, and of that of the Buddhists, which was still to form, we want to be able to say that what the Buddha was preaching and practising was religion. A similar argument can be presented in respect of Mohammed or Jesus. My conclusion, therefore, is that a definition of religion, if it is not to be unduly restrictive, must not include the requirement of a community. If I have succeeded in communicating clearly that the point I am making is of a logical nature, it will be seen that, appearances notwithstanding, Cantwell Smith may have in mind something different, although possibly related.[7]

Consequently, Ninian Smart's objections need not apply to what I am saying. Consider, for example, Smart's comment that

> although Cantwell Smith draws attention to the way in which faith may express itself in community relations, that is in the orientation of the individual to the community, he does not appear to have a place for actual communal religious acts or, if you like, communal responses to the transcendent. Just as only a group of people can conspire (an individual cannot do this on his own), so certain important religious acts can only be done by a group. This itself means that the analysis of a religious focus may have to take into account group activities, such as group ritual activities.[8]

The point made, particularly in the last two sentences, is a valid one. My response to this would be to say that the definition of religion is different from the 'analysis of a religious focus'; and, therefore, the fact that society or community is not integral to the former, does not entail that it may not be so to the analysis of a religious focus in relation to a particular religion. Indeed, where a religion does actually have a community, religiosity can only be actually characterised by analysing and noting the social (as well as personal) aspects of the experiences, beliefs, attitudes, actions and other commitments in question. The only thing I am arguing against is incorporating this social aspect into the definition of the concept of religion, and thus excluding rather more personal, 'eccentric' expressions of religiosity from being considered as examples of religion.

Let me now dispose of one other anticipated objection. It may be said that my definition seems to suggest that what is contained in the metaphysical theory will determine the believer's attitudes and actions. But the theory, it could be objected, would normally consist of descriptive claims about reality, and from these alone, judgments regarding how one ought to view certain things and, in particular, how one ought to behave, cannot be said to follow, for we know that an 'ought' cannot be derived from an 'is'. Three things are relevant here. Firstly, it is not self-evident why the statements of the theory need necessarily be pure descriptions: 'God loves his creatures', while descriptive in form, is meant to be evocative of certain attitudes and behaviour as well: in theories of the sort here in question facts and values are unlikely to be sharply distinct. Secondly, my definition does not require that the attitude-and-action-commitments do, as a matter of fact, follow from the theory, but only that they *be seen* by the believer to do so. Finally, it has to be said for whatever it is worth, that ethical naturalism, namely, the view that values cannot be derived from facts alone, is no less and no more justified than inductive inference. It was Hume who, in recent thought, first stressed the logical impropriety, if that's what it is, of deriving an 'ought' from an 'is', a view accepted by many philosophers in the period since Hume, even though it was Aristotle who first made the point. The selfsame Hume, however, also immortalised the so-called 'problem of induction', i.e. the non-derivability of universal laws and generalisations from mere statements about particulars. But this circumstance, that 'is' statements of a universal character, i.e. laws and accidental generalisations cannot strictly be derived from a collection of other 'is' statements, i.e. particular propositions, has not stopped scientific practice in important areas from formulating important 'laws of nature' inductively. And it seems that Hume notwithstanding, religious practice, likewise, has, in so far as it has, continued to derive value judgments from descriptions; and in so doing may have given ethical naturalism at least the 'pragmatic' justification that induction is supposed by many to have.

Now at last we come to consider the scope of my account, *extensionally*, i.e. how far it can be said to apply to religions other than Buddhism, regarded as paradigmatic in my account. It is not my intention to undertake this exercise in relation to every single religion: that would be neither possible, nor particularly profitable in view of my stated belief that no known religion seems to be excluded. I would, therefore, only look at Christianity and Hinduism to see if the outline sketched by me finds corroboration. Though the precise details of the early life of Jesus are shrouded in mystery, we know enough to be able to make the informed guess that he was somehow aware of his special role and vocation, fairly early in his life – perhaps at the age of twelve, when after being at last discovered to be still in the temple of Jerusalem, he is supposed to have said that he had special obligations to his Father. Awareness of this sort, strengthened from time to time by his perception that events in his life answered significant biblical prophecies, culminating perhaps in the alleged supernatural events taking place immediately after his baptism by St John, could be said to represent his unusual perception that he was someone special, perhaps divine – not a feeling that anyone could find less than deeply moving, even disturbing, and certainly puzzling. Significantly, the baptism, we are told, is followed by his 'stay' in the wilderness for a period of forty days, after which he publicly undertakes his ministry and displays, according to all accounts, a kind of 'authority' which had clearly been lacking before. It is not too fanciful to think that the difference between the Jesus before his disappearance into the wilderness and the one after, is that between a man who has had a profound 'vision' but who cannot yet put it into a meaningfully complete framework, and one who has resolved his conflicts and hesitations by seeing his vision as part of an explanatory, theoretical whole. Jesus before the wilderness phase could be said to be just a man with a powerful 'blik'; after it, he is one with a coherent set of 'revelations' or theoretical propositions: he 'knows' who he is, namely the incarnation of God, the son of God, the King of the Jews; he 'knows' what his obligations to the rest of the world are and what they owe him. The period in the wilderness could be said to mark off the high point of 'incubation' of his perceptions and ideas. The details, of course, are vastly different, but the pattern, I suggest, is not too unlike the course of life of the Buddha.

Hinduism, not being a prophetic religion, and not having a historically recorded point in time as its beginning, is somewhat harder to handle. But most scholars of Hinduism have noted the difference at least in the tone of the early parts of the Vedas and the later ones. Most of the early hymns have been seen as the spontaneous poetic outpourings of men who have experienced awe, intimacy, ecstasy and similar feelings in the presence of natural forces, e.g. fire, storm, thunder, lightning, water, etc., which are immediately identified with certain gods and goddesses who command worship and adulation. But these supernatural creatures do not, as it were, fit into a coherent whole. As a result, sometimes one and sometimes another of them is extolled as the highest among them, the controller of them all. But the identification of which of them, or what, if not they, provides the ultimate ground of everything, is a recurring problem, which finds expression in such Vedic verses as 'What God shall we adore with our oblations?'[9] This felt uncertainty often leads to open scepticism, even cynicism, such as in the 'Hymn of Creation', which raises searching questions about the origins of the world and the why and wherefore of it all; and ends as follows:

> This world-creation, whence it has arisen,
> Or whether it has been produced or not,
> He who surveys it in the highest heaven,
> He only knows or ev'n he does not know it.[10]

These poetic 'visions' and philosophical perplexities continue to alternate, not necessarily in equal proportion, until we come to the later Vedas, the Upanishads being their culmination, when the theoretical superstructure begins to emerge. While the Upanishads seldom lose the poetic fervour of the early Vedas, their tone and idiom are pre-eminently speculative, philosophical; and while there are many distinct theoretical perspectives suggested throughout the hundred-odd Upanishads, it is safe, I think, to say that the metaphysical doctrine of the unity of *Brahman* and *ātman* is the dominant one among them. At least so it has appeared to be to some of the most eminent Hindus down the centuries.

With this brief look at Christianity and Hinduism – very different types of religion, indeed – I would like to reaffirm my claim that the logical, though not necessarily chronological, pattern noticed in these two and in Buddhism, of course, namely, intensely personal experiences followed by, or accompanied with, metaphysical theories, can be found in the development of all religions. I know of nothing that makes this suggestion implausible. I find it hard to imagine that one could come up with the example of a religion, which, while recognised as such, did not actually fit the outline of certain kinds of experiences and a metaphysical theory along with the three types of commitment mentioned. If there are such counter-examples, I would naturally like to know of them. In the meantime, I like to think that the general concept of religion has found an adequate, and hopefully useful, explication.

Given the soundness of this assumption, it is not difficult to see what the outline of an adequate characterisation of specific religions would be like. It would, in my opinion, consist of a detailed description of the relevant experiences or 'visions', the metaphysical theory in question and the salient features of the three kinds of commitment involved, highlighting those unique features which tend to set it apart from other religions. This is where the differences relevant to the analysis and classification of different religions will show up. The different 'visions' or experiences of the world, the differences in the nature and details of the metaphysical and other beliefs and the distinguishing features of the nature and intensity of the three kinds of commitment, will enter into the analysis of the uniqueness of particular religions. This will be the place, too, for displaying the distinctively socialised ritual or other acts characteristic of a religion. And yet the rubric of such analysis and description would be provided by the general concept of religion explicated in the definition I have offered.

# 5 Does Religion Explain?

It has been held by many, philosophers as well as social scientists, that it is wrong or misleading to regard religious belief-systems as explanatory theories or hypotheses. Since this view, as well as its opposite, is closely tied to theories entertained about the nature of so-called religious language, a fuller discussion of the issues involved must await a subsequent chapter. In this chapter I intend to examine – in so far as this can be done relatively independently of other related issues – whether religion can be said to explain; and, if so, what and how. In particular, an attempt will be made to see whether religious doctrines resemble, either wholly or partly, scientific explanatory theories. But, first, it may be necessary to make two useful distinctions. The question, 'Does religion explain?' is different from 'Can religion be explained?' though the two may be related. The latter is about the 'justification of religion', and is often discussed as part of a reductionist or apologist platform, and is, therefore, not relevant to my descriptive task. The other distinction, of an entirely different kind, is the one between trying and succeeding in the context of explanation. 'Does religion attempt to explain?' is not the same question as 'Does it succeed in explaining whatever it purports to explain?' Indeed, a negative answer to the former may make the latter quite redundant. These distinctions, I suggest, will help avoid a few unnecessary confusions in the course of the discussion to follow.

I have already stated explicitly that, in my opinion, religious belief-systems, whatever else they might be, are explanatory, metaphysical theories.[1] They are intended and, at least partly, function as explanatory systems. Whether they can be said to succeed in explaining, according to given external criteria, is another matter; and in so far as it is legitimate to place this demand on religious theories, whether they do satisfy the conditions required is something we shall consider shortly. Also, my claim that religious systems are at least partly theories is not meant to imply that *for believers* they are tentative hypotheses awaiting confirmation or falsification. The deep commitment stipulated in my definition should rule out any tentativeness at the same time. But the fact that believers take the truth of their metaphysics for granted is quite consistent with the actual falsity, or unsoundness, of the system, viewed according to specified criteria. As I see it, then, an affirmative answer to the question, 'Does religion attempt to explain?' is quite consistent with a negative answer to 'Does it succeed in explaining whatever it sets out to explain?'

I will now try to answer the question what it is that religion can be said to explain. The simplest uncontroversial answer that can be given, I think, is that, like all other explanatory theories, it purports to explain *experience*, or something given in experience. Further specification, however, takes us clearly beyond the range of the uncontroversial. What kind or type, or quality, of experience does religion attempt to explain? In view of the fact that every known religion seems to incorporate a cosmology, of one sort or another, most people prepared to regard religious systems as explanatory at all, tend to take the view that it explains ordinary experience, namely, our experience of events or processes in the natural world: why these should be the way they seem to be. The relevant evidence from religions does not, in my opinion, by itself warrant a clear judgment that this view is entirely false; nor, on the other hand, that there is nothing wrong with it. Religious communities do seem to give the impression that their beliefs about, and attitudes and responses to the world are largely legitimised by appealing to the cosmology and system of values implicit in their religions. Particular statements of their belief-systems many on occasions be given a symbolic interpretation; but, by and large, the system operates as a (to them) coherent whole, incorporating not only an ontology but also a set of values, which together determine their perception of and response to particular events. Prayer, worship, ritual homage and sacrifice offered in the name of the transcendental entities would otherwise not be seen as having the power to bring about desired consequences; success and failure of individual action would otherwise not be attributed to the pleasure or displeasure of the celestial powers, as it undoubtedly is in most religions, although in varying degrees.

On the other hand, though, such ritual action is seldom seen as a substitute for whatever common sense or science shows to be the proper means for the attainment of a given goal. Hunting is not abandoned in favour of prayer; farming is not relegated to the

## Does Religion Explain? 49

offering of flowers; and copulation with a view to begetting children is not dispensed with in the hope of virgin births. Had prayer, worship and ritual replaced instrumental action dictated by the normal perception of causes and effects, there would then be good grounds for saying that religion performed entirely and exactly the same functions as science and common sense. My feeling, therefore, is that religion is best seen as an activity parallel to but different from science. It explains not the world of ordinary experience or that of common sense, but rather that as appearing in extraordinary experiences by unique individuals, peculiar when first experienced but from then on capable of serving as moulds of perception for others. It is as though figures like the Buddha, Christ and Mohammed had succeeded in producing revolutionary, new pairs of glasses: once put on, the world never looks the same again. But precisely because the world takes on a completely new character, it requires to be explained, to be put into a new conceptual framework. I would like to maintain, therefore, that it is such special perceptions, or 'bliks', that religion attempts to explain. I would not want to argue that religion never or in no way tries to explain common sense perception or experience at all: the normal and the religious perceptions of the world must obviously overlap. It is possible that in 'traditional', or so-called 'primitive' religions, this overlap is much greater; so that common sense, science and religion are all inextricably mixed in a loose but comprehensive system. But 'modern' religions, i.e. the world religions of the Middle East, China and India are, in my opinion, better understood as arising primarily from the need to explain these special insights. For in these countries, at least, we encounter considerable growth of science and technology at the same time, which makes it harder to take the view that religion was seen as having precisely the same function as science. In my opinion, therefore, as we move from traditional to modern religions we notice a gradual switch from the explanation of ordinary, everyday experience to that of special experiences, or rather of the appearance of things as determined by such experiences.

A word now needs to be said about the model of explanation usually employed in religion. The best that comes to my mind is the analogy of a picture-puzzle. If one happens accidentally to get hold of one of the pieces from such a puzzle, one is unlikely at first to understand fully why it should have that peculiar but interesting shape; and if the curiosity is intense, one would not be content until the puzzle has been solved by putting all the pieces together and thus seeing precisely where the piece fits in the whole picture. The feeling of Jesus that he might be God, and, therefore, in a special relationship to people and to the world, or that of the Buddha that the world was a 'veil' of suffering from which escape must be found, are, I suggest, analogous to the finding of the piece from the puzzle. Since the initial experience is not just a passing idle feeling, but, on the contrary, sustained and full of profound implications, the subject of such experiences is baffled, shaken, transformed. He cannot rest until the why and wherefore of the experience are revealed through a coherent set of suppositions, or 'revelations', as the case might be, a theory, which imparts significance and credibility to the experience. The pattern of explanation in religion would typically, therefore, seem to be a mixture of the causal and the teleological. Not only does the theory purport to subsume the data of experience in a causal network of transcendental entities, states and processes; but also provides guidance about the purpose behind the world and how man is to serve this purpose. The fact that the entities, etc. presupposed in the emerging cosmology are transcendental, and hence 'unseen' and unfamiliar, does not by itself render the theory non-explanatory. It is widely recognised now that explaining the familiar in terms of the unfamiliar is the rule rather than the exception in science. The law of gravitation is, to most people, far less familiar than the free fall of bodies it is supposed to explain; and the fundamentals of relativity theory are, by comparison with the phenomenon it explains, almost truly 'transcendental'. That the explanans be familar, in a psychological sense, is neither a necessary nor a sufficient condition for an explanation to be acceptable; and, therefore, the metaphysical nature of the theory in religion does not *per se* disqualify it as attempted explanation. Even if 'scientific explanation' is regarded as the paradigm of all explanations – although it is not self-evident why it should be – the sense in which religion can be said to explain must at least have a 'family-resemblance' to the former. This will become clearer, I hope, as we go along.

In view of the remarks made above, especially the last one, it may be desirable now to see what the requirements of explanation, especially scientific, are. This should enable a proper assessment of whether and to what extent religion can be said to explain. It has to be mentioned at the outset that even in science there is no single form of explanation uniformly offered or accepted, if only because there are many different sciences, at varying stages of development and with somewhat different goals. At the very least, there are three kinds: the causal, the historical and the teleological. Although there have been attempts to reduce the last two to the first, I am convinced that they remain distinct, each one of them required in its own right even in science, not to mention in other areas of enquiry. The Darwinian account of evolution is hardly causal in any strict sense; and much of the explaining in the social sciences is nothing if not teleological. It is not just that in certain areas of enquiry the non-causal forms of explanation are somehow more appropriate: the strict requirements of a causal model simply cannot be met in these areas. This brings us to the specification of these requirements.

The best known model of causal explanation perhaps is the one that has come to be called the 'deductive-nomological' model.[2] In this somewhat 'ideal' form, the explanandum is shown to follow deductively from the conjunction of a major premise expressing a universal law and a minor premise consisting of a set of antecedent conditions. So, if the phenomenon to be explained is: 'Why does that part of the oar which is under water appear to be bent upwards?' the explanation would consist of two sets of statements. The first set would contain certain general laws, for example, the law of refraction, and that water is an optically denser medium than air; while the second set would specify the antecedent conditions, e.g. that part of the oar was in water and part in air, and that the oar was a practically straight piece of wood or metal, as the case might be. The explanation here takes the form of an argument to the effect that given those laws and those initial conditions, the part of the oar under water *had* to look bent, because this is entailed by the combination of the law statements and the statements of antecedent conditions. The logical conditions of adequacy would thus seem to be the following: (1) the explanandum must be logically deducible from the explanans; (2) the explanans must contain general laws which are actually required for the derivation; and (3) the explanans must have empirical content, i.e. it must, in principle at least, be capable of test by observation and experiment. It is evident that if the last condition is not satisfied, the explanation could hardly claim to be scientific. To these three is added the extra, empirical condition of adequacy, namely (4) that the sentences constituting the explanans must be true. For if any of them is false, then the premises taken together would be false; and from false premises one cannot validly deduce a true conclusion, i.e. the explanandum which describes an actual event. Since the truth or falsity of scientific laws, however, is dependent on the acceptability or otherwise, at a given time, of the relevant theories; and since we know that certain theories and laws once regarded as true are no longer so, it would seem sensible to interpret condition (4) epistemically, and so acknowledge an epistemic condition, namely (5) that the explanans must be *known* to be true, at the relevant time, for it to constitute an acceptable explanation. But, thus stated, this condition may be too strong: for what may be 'known' to be true at one time may turn out to be false later, thus leading to the odd consequence that what might have once been a 'true' explanation turned out in fact to be false. But this is an unsatisfactory use of the word 'true': what is really true should remain so. The best way of avoiding these difficulties, therefore, may be to state condition (5) in a weaker form and say that the explanans must not be known to be false. But this amounts to no more than the modest claim that the explanans must be *believed* to be true, on the basis of available evidence, of course.

This deductive-nomological model which, along with the 'probabilistic', is called the 'covering-law' model of explanation, has often, and rightly, been regarded as having a rather limited scope: in the biological and social sciences teleological and functional explanations are seen to abound: and even in the physical sciences examples are not hard to come by where explanation is not strictly deductive-nomological. Critics of the model have pointed out instances of perfectly acceptable explanation which either do not contain laws, do not require statements of antecedent conditions or, worse, do not satisfy the requirement of strict deducibility of the explanandum from the explanans; or again whose 'law-statements' are not strictly true, but considered at a given time to be highly probable. Thus, if the critics are right, none of the conditions of adequacy seems, taken singly, to be necessary. Let us take examples of each of these 'deviant' cases. If we explain why a person contracted measles by pointing out that he was in the company of someone else with measles, it should count as a perfectly acceptable explanation, even though it is not a law that one person with measles will necessarily transmit the infection to another in his company. Sometimes laws themselves require to be explained in terms of other laws and theories, and in these cases no antecedent conditions need to be stated: for example, Kepler's laws of planetary motion can be explained by showing that they are derivable from the principles of Newtonian physics. In the case of so-called 'probabilistic' explanations, the explanandum is not strictly entailed by the explanans; for the 'law' involved only states a statistical probability rather than universal and uniform concomitance of events of two kinds. Also, and finally, these statistical 'laws' are not true, but only highly confirmed and, therefore, have a high degree of probability only. Although they are not known to be false, they could, in principle, be so.

The reason for labouring with this point about the limitations of this model is to show that even within scientific practice it is regarded more as an ideal form which it is desirable for explanations to approximate, rather than as one which is invariably adopted. It is only to be expected, then, that the rather demanding conditions imposed by this model are hardly likely to be met anywhere outside of certain natural sciences. And that goes for religion as well. It should be sufficient, I think, if the explanations proffered in religion were to show a broad similarity of pattern wherever appropriate; and this, it seems to me, is the case. Starting with the epistemic condition, it needs no arguing that the propositions together constituting the equivalent of the explanans are believed to be true! I have already argued that religious people take the truth of their belief-system for granted, rather than as awaiting verification. This very fact, however, raises a serious problem regarding the condition of testability. For it is clear that, since for believers their theory is not a provisional hypothesis, they obviously do not *intend* to subject their beliefs to deliberate attempts at verification or falsification. Consequently, in this sense, religious explanations do not meet the testability condition: they seem to remain true irrespective of facts. But too much must not be made of this appearance; for whatever their intentions, it is not rare for believers to find their beliefs making excessive demands on their credibility. A kind of 'subterranean' testing, I would like to maintain, goes on all the same. A fuller examination of this thesis will be undertaken in a later chapter.

Going back to the logical conditions, there seems little doubt in my mind that particular happenings acquire their significance, or particular courses of action are seen as obligatory by the believer, because they *seem to follow* from the very general truths – 'laws', if you like – contained in their belief-systems; and, what is more, the believers, on certain occasions at least, may be fully aware that only in their religious view do the happenings in question have that significance and the actions their obligatory character. In short, as far as the believers' awareness goes, the derivability condition, that requiring that some statements of the explanans be of law-like generality, and that these 'laws' be actually required for the derivation, would all seem, in effect, to be satisfied. Whether strict logical entailment obtains; whether the broad principles used in the explanation can be really called laws; whether these are really testable and, if so, whether they can 'objectively' be said to be true – these, and many others, are questions that arise only in the context of asking whether the proffered explanations of religion do succeed in doing what they set out to do. These questions cannot be settled easily, if indeed they can be settled at all. They raise much larger, almost intractable, theoretical issues some of which, it is hoped, will be discussed in later chapters. For the time being, however, I hope it is safe to conclude that in intent at least religious theories must be explanatory; and also that, again in intent, they sometimes have the broad character of the most demanding form of causal explanations.

Perhaps one or two examples of actual explanation in religion are called for in support of my claim. Some idea of the way in which the overall 'visions' or 'bliks' of Buddhism, Christianity and Hinduism could be said to be explained by subsumption under the relevant theoretical structures of metaphysical beliefs, has already been conveyed in the previous chapter in the course of the examination of the scope of my definition. Let us, therefore, now take some examples of a different sort. Suppose that the 'red light' district of a city, inhabited, supposedly, by pimps, prostitutes and criminals, suffers particular devastation as a result of an earthquake in the area. Scientists later determine that the epicentre of the earthquake was located close to the area, which, for scientific purposes adequately explains why it should have suffered greater damage. One can, however, easily imagine a certain sort of Christian taking the view that the destruction of that area was the result of God's wrath provoked by the sins committed there. For such a person, the location of the epicentre there is not an explanation but the very fact to be explained. The reason why this happened is that God *caused* it to happen that way. If necessary, one can roughly delineate the formal deductive structure of the argument underlying the explanation as follows:

Explanans { God always punishes sin (the 'law')
That part of the city was living sinfully (the antecedent condition)

Explanandum $\left\{\begin{array}{l}\text{ . . . God punished it by locating the epi-}\\ \text{centre of the earthquake there (which}\\ \text{caused the damage and destruction).}\end{array}\right.$

The fact that this explanation fails to account for the suffering of those living in the area who were in fact virtuous or that sinners elsewhere escaped the punishment, may make it a bad or unacceptable explanation. But this is relevant to the success or failure of the ostensible explanation, and does not alter the fact that one was offered, in terms of a religious doctrine, apparently in the causal model. Or take the case of the Hindu who notices inequalities in the conditions of individuals in his society, namely, that some are born rich and others poor, some in 'high' and others in 'low-caste' families; the parents of some are virtuous, 'wise' people, while those of others are 'wicked' and ignorant. For him these facts are not just fortuitous: the conditions of birth, including the dispositions one is born with, are determined by one's *karmas*, one's deeds in previous lives. Why an individual is born poor, or why he is so inextricably attached to earthly pleasures is the result of the inexorable 'Law' of *Karma*. Thus the explanation of such events or phenomena is in terms of this 'Law' and the supposition that the individual concerned must in his previous life have performed actions which warranted punishment (or reward) as expressed in the circumstances of his birth. The 'Law' of *Karma* and the antecedent conditions in the form of the supposed actions of the individual in a previous life together explain 'facts' about his present life. Once again, the objection that this sort of explanation does not uniquely explain any particular state of affairs, and could be used to explain one of an indefinite number of phenomena equally plausibly (or implausibly), while crucial to the truth (falsity) of the explanation, does nothing to affect its status as a proffered explanation with an identifiable formal structure, namely, the causal.

But even if this were not the case, the claim that religious theories are used for explanatory purposes will not have been debunked. For we have noted that even in science there are historical, and teleological explanations, the conditions of adequacy for which are much less stringent and would, therefore, be easily satisfied by the relevant kinds of explanation offered in religion. Besides, in religion there is undoubtedly a great deal of what Scriven calls[3] 'horizontal explanation' (analogy, correlation, etc.) as against 'vertical explanation' (derivation) forms which are none the less explanatory. Explaining, in ordinary parlance, has a lot of context-dependence. Who needs the explanation, and under what circumstances, largely determines what would count as one. The basic purpose of explaining is to make someone understand what he did not understand before; and this understanding and the consequent feeling of psychological satisfaction can be brought about in many different ways. It needs no arguing that explanation in this ordinary sense is a task demanded of religion and performed successfully, in my opinion, in numerous ways and on countless occasions.

Since I have argued, successfully I hope, that religious belief-systems have an explanatory character, I need immediately to discuss a related issue. Those who regard religions as explanatory theories usually think that such theories are pseudo-scientific systems of belief, which, like science, are designed to predict and control nature. The assumption made generally is that religion is the product of a pre-scientific mentality, and hence only in a society *without* proper science and technology can it possibly have any useful role. Now in so far as this is a clearly reductionist thesis, I do not, for that reason, intend to take much interest in it. But what I do need to consider is whether religious theories are intended to acquire control and mastery over nature and, therefore, have predictive as well as explanatory functions. There is little doubt, to my mind, that part at least of most religions, perhaps a large part of traditional religion at any rate, does *seem* to have this instrumental goal. Supernatural agencies of various sorts are invoked, cajoled and appeased in various ways for bringing about desired goals. Reference was made to this phenomenon earlier in this chapter. But I also felt obliged to point out that too literal an interpretation of such phenomena as praying for rain or for sons, ritual performances apparently designed to further either terrestial or other-worldly goals, presents certain anomalies. For even in the most traditional of societies, with next to no systematic science or technology, such religious acts have seldom been substitutes for appropriate instrumental action, e.g. hunting, farming, or what have you. This was very forcefully brought out by Wittgenstein[4] who went on to point out how curious it was that those African tribes, for example, who appealed to the 'rain-King' for rain, always did so when the rainy season had come, and not at other times. If prayer or a ritual dance or sacrifice was really supposed by these people to bring about rain, they would be expected to be asking for it whenever they pleased. Whether, therefore, these actions were designed to control nature becomes questionable even in the context of traditional religions.

As we move towards modern religions, there seems to be a visible departure from treating religious ritual or prayer as instruments to earthly goals; although, in my opinion, the tendency never quite disappears. More importantly, we find that in many modern religions there is a clear, sometimes strong, tendency to belittle and transcend merely earthly goals: control over nature hardly seems to be a preoccupation of some of the most admired religious saints and mystics. But the desire to understand or intuit the mysteries behind nature either through philosophical speculation or mystic vision or through God's grace and revelation seems to persist across cultures. Equally, the idea of control, in so far as it is encountered, is not so much control of nature as of one's own self and its destiny. The elaborate forms of self-discipline practised by Yogis and Zen masters can only on very special interpretation be seen as the attempt to control nature. One can imagine an argument to the effect that these forms of self-discipline are designed to achieve control over the body-mind complex which, of course, is part of nature. But it seems to me that while this interpretation can be defended to an extent, it nevertheless misses, in a very important way, the point of the self-discipline in question; which is not control over anything, but rather the discovery of the 'real' self and its relationship to whatever is considered ultimately real about or behind the world. The suggestion, therefore, that religion is about the control of nature is either entirely false or, at best, suspect. Whether this implies that perhaps religious assertions ought to be taken not as descriptions but rather as symbolic expressions of a unique form of life, is a question that we will have to discuss later when we come to the consideration of problems relating to the interpretation of 'religious language'. In the meantime, and merely as a brief anticipation, I want to say that I do not find the arguments against a (by and large) literal interpretation of 'religious language' compelling. If I did, I would not have been arguing for the view that religious belief-systems are explanatory theories. My brief conclusion regarding the question at hand, then, is that these theories can legitimately be seen as either only having the function of explaining or producing understanding; or else, if they must have some other goal, then the goal must be stated in terms likely to include much more than mere control of nature. 'Coming to terms with the world', especially as seen through the relevant 'vision' or 'bliks', and perhaps 'preparing oneself for the ultimate (transcendental) destiny', seem to me much more likely to accommodate the many variations among religions in respect of what they are supposed to do for believers.

At least one major objection can be anticipated at this point. A well-known view prevalent among philosophers of science is that explanation and prediction have the same logical structure,[5] though the latter is directed towards the future and the former towards the past. This in effect means, it is claimed, that an adequate explanation is also at the same time a basis for an actual or potential prediction, and vice versa. If this is true, then an argument can be easily developed to show that, in so far as I regard religious theories to be explanatory, I cannot dissociate myself from the claim that they must also have a predictive function, and hence serve the purpose of control over nature. Many things can be said in answer. But, without going into the technical details of a different area of enquiry, i.e. philosophy of science, I will just say the following. To start with, the claim about the logical identity of explanation and prediction is made only in respect of science and so can only be true there, if anywhere at all. I have merely tried to draw parallels between the patterns of explanation in science and religion, but explicitly maintained that, similarities in certain respects notwithstanding, they are different enterprises. Thus expectations that can be legitimately entertained in one area would be quite out of place in the other. Secondly, examples given earlier in this chapter show quite clearly, I think, that the alleged symmetry between explanation and prediction does not hold even in science. The Darwinian theory of evolution is considered a sound explanation of certain features of the origin of species, but no one, least of all Darwin, would dream of predicting, for example, what the shape or size of the next species to evolve would be. Conversely, enough seems to be known statistically about the connection between cigarette-smoking and lung cancer for us to find plausible the prediction that someone smoking, say, two hundred cigarettes a day would be very likely to get lung cancer; but it is unlikely that this would be seen as doing much towards dispelling our ignorance about what it is that causes cancer and how. The supposed symmetry between explanation and prediction, therefore, is an ideal which it may be hoped all, or most, scientific explanations might eventually approximate; it is not a reality which obtains outside of the physical, and certain other 'advanced' sciences.[6] Consequently, it cannot do much for the argument, indirect as it already is, that religion aims at the control of nature. But I hope to have shown that, in a very legitimate sense, religion can be said to explain.

# 6 Believing and Understanding

There is an obvious connection between believing and understanding which needs to be made explicit. Normally, if someone says that he believes such and such, we expect that he understands what he believes. It would strike us as odd if we were told that he definitely believes something but does not quite understand it; even more so if he claimed not to understand it at all. In such cases what we would wish to say, at the very least, is that the belief in question is irrational. We may even wish to take the view that the person concerned merely *says* he believes such and such but cannot really be considered actually to do so. Understanding, thus, seems to be a precondition of believing. Is there a case also for saying that believing is a precondition of understanding? Some philosophers seem to want to give an affirmative answer to this question. If they are right, then we get into the curious position that believing and understanding are both preconditions of each other. But, curious or not, this position easily leads to the one held by certain philosophers, notably, D. Z. Phillips,[1] that believing and understanding are identical, that one cannot do one without doing the other at the same time. Failure in one is *eo ipse* failure in the other as well. These views – namely, the identity of believing and understanding, or that believing is a precondition of understanding, as also its converse, have had a confused history. Hence the need to examine them closely.

Since the confusion has been especially rampant in the context of religion, it is perhaps helpful to stay clear of this area until the conceptual boundaries of the two terms have been mapped out a little in general. Starting with belief, it is perhaps safe to say that one can legitimately ask two distinct questions: (a) 'What causes X to believe that $p$?'; and (b) 'How can we tell that he does actually believe that $p$?' There is at least a third, important, question too: namely, (c) 'Is X's belief true or false?' But we will postpone questions regarding truth/falsity of beliefs, in so far as this is possible, until the next chapter. In answer to (a)-type questions, the believer may either list causes or conditions of his belief or may give other reasons (every reason is not necessarily causal) why he believes that a certain state of affairs obtained. 'Why do you believe that there is a fire burning inside that house?' is adequately answered by 'Because I can see smoke rising through the chimney', for there is an invariable concomitance between fire and smoke. Such an answer would normally satisfy us that the person questioned understands what he believes, for he is fully aware of the relationship between smoke and fire. This fact of the believer understanding what is involved in his answer has an important bearing on the (b)-type questions, namely, those relating to the evidence for someone believing such and such. For if the believer understands what it is that he believes, then, and only then, would his belief be expected to make a difference to his actions. If a person says that he believes the bull standing in the field is dangerous, but seems to show no sign of caution, or, worse, seems to be doing everything likely to arouse the bull's fury, then we will say that he does not believe that the bull is dangerous, unless, of course, we have reason to suspect that he is out on a 'suicide mission'.

Can one be said to believe something one does not understand? It would seem to be odd to say so, for in that case, the alleged believer would neither be able to tell us why he believes it, nor would he be expected to show any signs in his behaviour which could distinguish him from someone who believed the opposite? Believing that something is the case entails being aware that something else could not be, or is not, the case. If I believe that the earth is round, then I cannot at the same time believe it to be square. I cannot believe the earth to be round and yet also fear that if I kept walking indefinitely long and straight in a given direction, I would fall off it. It is evident that to believe something is to understand the implications of the belief: what else it may or may not be consistent with. We may not be able to judge the coherence of one of our beliefs with *all* our other beliefs: this may indeed be humanly impossible; but we must at least be aware of its congruence or otherwise with certain closely related ones. Not to know even what these might be, is not to understand what one purports to believe and, therefore, is not to believe it.

This general relation between believing and understanding, namely, that the latter is a condition of the former, is often claimed to have either no application or a very limited one in the context of religion. It has been argued since the earliest times by 'fideist' theologians that, while in the context of rational discourse one may not be said to believe something without understanding it, religious belief is not rational discourse; and hence questions of evidence, reasoning, proof, and the like do not arise here. In religion one accepts certain things 'on faith', and not because there is compelling evidence or clinching arguments for them. Various degrees of fideism have been associated with St Paul, J. G. Hamann, Montaigne, Bayle, Sören Kierkegaard, and others.[2] In its extreme form fideism claims that far from believing something because we understand it, faith requires the acceptance of certain things because they are absurd. Tertullian's dictum *credo quia absurdum* (I believe that which is absurd) is taken as the guiding light here. This position has been aptly summed up by Hume's ironic statement at the end of his essay 'Of Miracles':

> *Christian Religion* not only was at first attended with miracles, but even to this day cannot be believed by any reasonable person without them. Mere reason is not sufficient to convince us of its veracity; and whoever is moved by *Faith* to assent to it, is conscious of a continued miracle in his own person, which subverts all the principles of his understanding, and gives him a determination to believe what is most contrary to custom and experience.[3]

The intended irony in Hume's statement of the position notwithstanding, many fideists have praised Hume's formulation of the essence of faith. Had the claims of Christianity been altogether rational and plausible, one's decision to commit oneself to its precepts would not have involved the fear and trembling that, according to Kierkegaard, for example, is characteristic of 'the leap into faith'.[4]

Moderate fideists like Augustine and Pascal, on the other hand, take the view that while it is through faith that one is enabled to make the choice of ultimate truths, reason is not altogether irrelevant. The explanation, and even the initial search, for these is helped by the latter. The anti-rationalism here does not deny the important role of reason, but insists that there are strong limits to rational enquiry: and hence in the end the choice of ultimate truths must rest on faith. The guiding maxim here is Augustine's *credo ut intelligam* (I believe in order to know).[5] According to this view, reason both precedes and succeeds faith. This moderate form of fideism, it seems to me, does not deny the need to attempt to understand what we believe, nor our partial success in doing so. What it seems to deny is our ability to comprehend completely the nature of ultimate truth and our ability to justify rationally the choice of truth we make. In its latter aspect, it may be of a piece with the kind of view taken by scientists and philosophers in the context of choosing one from competing scientific theories: the final choice of one among competing scientific theories is not itself made by rational criteria but rather by aesthetic ones, such as simplicity and symmetry, or by considerations of economy and complexity, sometimes even criteria of a moral and religious kind. This kind of fideism, it would seem, does not challenge the view that we must understand – at least to a limited extent – what we believe; it merely recognises limits to rational enquiry and its role in our lives. I do not regard that as an indefensible position and there seems to be nothing in it which could be said to be inconsistent with the view of religion I have tried to outline in earlier chapters.

The extreme form of fideism, however, seems to me to be false in the wider context of all religions, and is probably so in the Christian context as well. Faith may involve a 'leap' in the end, but it seems to me that it is usually preceded by an attempt to understand the nature and implications of the belief. This understanding may be either in general, rational terms or only in terms of the metaphysical theory enjoined by the religion in question. There may be – indeed are – certain concepts in every religion which are declared the area of mystery: a Christian may not claim to understand why God works the way he does; the Hindu may speak of *Brahman* as the one 'where the eye goes not nor speech nor hearing', etc; the Jew may not understand why he is God's 'elect'. But by and large a religious believer certainly seems to understand what he believes. The Christian's belief in resurrection would not constitute a 'leap' unless he was aware of the miraculous nature of the event; the Hindu's belief in reincarnation is not an exercise in incomprehension: if it were, he would not, as he does, refer to evidence for rebirth, nor produce, as he does, rational arguments for his belief. The Jew understands perfectly what his belief in the prophethood of Isaiah means and so does the Muslim about the prophethood of Mohammed. The Christian seems to know what he believes when he claims that Jesus was 'made God'; and the Hindu appears to comprehend what's involved in the claim that Rama or Krishna were incarnations of Vishnu. It is because these religious people understand what they believe that their beliefs play significant roles in their lives; that is why these beliefs manage to explain to them events and facts that would otherwise remain inexplicable and incredible. To claim that certain items of faith take us beyond reason is not to claim that all religious beliefs are in principle non-rational. The amount of rational debate and controversy in the history of religions demonstrates the attempt by each religion to understand in rational terms what one or another of their beliefs amounted to. Rational theology, of whichever kind, may not have succeeded in establishing the existence of the transcendental entities, etc. presupposed by the relevant religions, but the attempt has consistently, and everywhere, been made.

The discussion so far in this chapter has been intended to show that, notwithstanding the contrary claims of traditional fideism, believing does indeed entail understanding, as much in religion as elsewhere. Let us now look at the converse side of the 'equation', and ask 'Is understanding necessarily believing?' In other words, can we not understand without believing, as seems to be held or suggested by many? Once again, we will offer a preliminary, general analysis before examining views about it in the context of religion. It seems that, as in the case of believing, one may also in the case of a purported claim to understand, ask: 'He says he does, but does he really?' What will settle this question one way or the other may be the same sorts of things that are relevant in showing that someone really believes something; i.e. the evidence for both may be appropriate kinds of behaviour. If someone truly understands that the wall in front of him is made of solid stones, we will not expect him to try to walk through it; if questioned about it, he will be expected to say things about the wall that do convey reasonably clearly that he knows in what important ways stones behave differently from, say, water or air. Appropriate behaviour – linguistic and other – is the evidence for someone understanding a certain proposition, as it is for believing it. This in turn involves knowledge of some of the implications and presuppositions of the proposition in question. Where the understanding may be said to be primarily of a non-propositional kind – those activities that Ryle characterised as examples of 'knowing how',[6] e.g. the ability to play chess or ride a bicycle – the evidence that a person really understands may lie almost entirely in his non-linguistic 'performance' or behaviour.

The symmetry between the 'logic' of believing and understanding, however, does not seem to go much beyond this reference to behaviour as evidence. For a start, the very trivial point to be noted is that, while it is perfectly legitimate to ask why one believes something, it does not make any sense to ask why one understands it. Only in the case of a failure to understand may one be expected to give reasons why; that is, what it was that made one *mis*understand the proposition, gesture or other symbol in question. More importantly, understanding does not necessarily entail believing: not everything we understand need be believed. False propositions will be *dis*believed precisely because they are understood. Only in the case of true propositions, therefore, may one say that to understand is to believe; and even here there may be said to be exceptions. For instance, a proposition may in fact be true but I might not know it to be so and hence not believe it; or I may, for example, know the facts establishing the infidelity of my beloved, and yet refuse to believe it – a paradigm case perhaps of the head affirming but the heart disavowing the same state of affairs. It would seem, then, that in general believing is not a precondition of understanding, nor does the latter presuppose the former.

But, once again, religion is claimed to be an exception. Just as traditional fideism denies that believing is understanding, so contemporary fideism of a particular variety affirms that understanding is believing. This particular brand has been nicknamed 'Wittgensteinian fideism'; and its supporters or exponents include such names as Winch, Hughes, Malcolm, Geach, Phillips and others, not to mention Wittgenstein himself (although it is questionable if he would have wholeheartedly supported some of the interpretations of his ideas put forward by his followers). This modern fideism incorporates a variety of claims, some of which have been spelt out by Kai Nielsen in his paper, 'Wittgensteinian fideism'.[7] Its central plank, however, is that religion is a distinct 'form of life', with its own distinct form of language. Each distinct form of life, it is held, has its own internal logic; and it is odd and improper to evaluate the contents of one form of life by the application of criteria borrowed from another. Understanding a form of life is only possible if one becomes a 'participant' in it. Since participation, it is sometimes alleged, implies acceptance of the relevant form of life, it follows that for a proper understanding of the form of life one has to believe the items constituting it.

It must be confessed that, even among Wittgensteinians, rarely does this thesis take the explicit form of a straightforward identity, although it does happen, as we shall see later. The majority seem only to emphasise clear awareness of the relevant form of life and its own internal logic as a condition of understanding; and hardly anyone thinks that a proper understanding of religion can be had without taking into account how the community of believers views a particular religious claim or practice. The last one of these shades of neo-Wittgensteinian opinion is, to my mind, quite reasonable and does not need any elaborate defence. What a proposition in physics really means can, after all, be hardly determined independently of how physicists understand it; and it is only sensible to hold that what religious utterances mean cannot, or should not, be ascertained without some reference to practitioners of the religion in question. The view that requires careful examination here is the one that believing is a necessary condition of understanding. For if this is shown to be false, then surely the stronger thesis of identity will fall with it.

The problem here is that the claim that belief is a necessary condition of understanding is hardly ever spelt out or defended explicitly as a general epistemological thesis. It is generally left in the air as an important implication of the overall doctrine we identified as Wittgensteinian fideism. The only general epistemological thesis which could be said to have a significant bearing on the issue now under consideration, and which has received ample elaboration and subsequent discussion and criticism, is to be found in some of the works of Peter Winch.[8] Indeed, it is partly because of this that Winch is included among fideists of the kind just mentioned. It has to be added, however, that, as far as I can see, Winch himself does not explicitly claim that one must believe in order to understand. In fact, at least once, he explicitly concedes the contrary when, after defending the view 'that the understanding of society cannot be observational and experimental in one widely accepted sense', he goes on to say this: 'What I am saying needs qualification. I do not mean, of course, that it is impossible to take as a datum that a certain person, or group of people, holds a certain belief – say that the earth is flat – without subscribing to it oneself.'[9] Winch seems to me to have something wider, and different, in mind. He is primarily arguing against the possibility, espoused by sociologists like Durkheim, Pareto and Weber, of pursuing social studies on the model of natural science. In this effort, according to Winch, some sociologists, e.g. Pareto, remove from their subject-matter 'precisely that which gives them sociological interest: namely their internal connection with a way of living'.[10] Furthermore, Winch argues, as against, say, anthropologists like Evans-Pritchard, that it is wrong to think that the beliefs of, for example, the Azande are irrational or superstitious simply because they do not square with modern scientific beliefs. To say that there can be no such things as witches or magic because science has shown these beliefs to be false, is to make the mistake of thinking that science, and only science, represents objective 'reality'; and that, therefore, all other forms of life must be judged rational or irrational strictly according to scientific criteria of rationality. But science, Winch (and many others) would wish to argue, is only one form of rationality and so only one of the many ways of determining what may or may not be real. According to him, religion and science are distinct modes of social life:

> . . . each has criteria of intelligibility peculiar to itself. So within science or religion actions can be logical or illogical: in science, for example, it would be illogical to refuse to be bound by the results of a properly carried out experiment; in religion it would be illogical to suppose that one could pit one's own strength against God's; and so on. But we cannot sensibly say that either the practice of science itself or that of religion is either illogical or logical: both are non-logical.[11]

In other words, what a religious claim amounts to can only be understood in the context of the religion in question.

In spite of the relativism implicit in this approach, there is much in it that can only be considered salutary and much required wisdom. It at least has the merit of not anointing as 'objective truth' what may only be particular religious and cultural opinions and dogmas. If only this wisdom had been available to missionary zealots of the past, much mischief, cruelty and bloodshed could have been avoided. As a warning against hasty judgments on forms of life to which we are strangers, Winch's view is commendable. But does it also follow that unless we subscribe to a particular belief-system, we may never understand it at all? I doubt that it does and it seems that Winch does so too. If believing is a condition of understanding, then I must believe everything I can be said to understand. But this is surely false. In the course of our general analysis of the relationship between believing and understanding, we noted that only when true propositions are involved can we be said to be obliged to believe what we understand, without being considered irrational; and there seems to be no reason to make religion an exception. I may legitimately be said to understand a Greek, Azande, Christian or pagan rite if I can perform all these moves in the correct sequence, and without prompting; and especially, if I know exactly what significance the rite has in the life of the relevant community. It should not be necessary for me actually to become – if this is possible – a Greek, Azande, Christian or pagan if I am not already one; and to insist on this requirement would seem to be an unnecessary and undesirable piece of linguistic legislation relating to the sense of 'understanding'. There is a rather more telling way of making this point, too. The bulk of published literature on 'primitive' cultures has been produced by Europeans. Since they continued to remain Europeans after all their scholarly dissertations had been written, they evidently had not changed their belief-systems and become Azandes or Trobriands. If the 'understanding is believing' thesis is true, then these scholars obviously did not understand the strange cultures they were writing their volumes on; and if they did, then clearly it is possible to understand without believing.

This objection can in fact be put even more strongly. Not only is it unnecessary to believe in order to understand; in certain contexts it may indeed be better not to do so. While there is one sense in which in order to understand we must get 'inside the circle' (i.e. participate, believe, etc in the given form of life), there is another in which we can only be said to understand if we are 'outside the circle'. It is true that understanding of a certain sort cannot be gained without requisite feelings of empathy or sympathy: we must be able to put ourselves in the 'shoes' or place of the believer. But the reverse of the coin surely is that just to the extent we are sympathetic to the believer and his culture, we may be failing to be 'impartial observers', without bias, without fear of being misjudged as to our motives. The latter may be said to be the condition of what might be called 'objective' understanding. Whether the demand of empathy can go hand in hand with the requirements of objectivity, is a question we will examine in the context of whether relativism and realism can be reconciled. In the meantime, I simply wish to affirm that for a full understanding of any form of life – religion, magic, science or art – both kinds of understanding, i.e. the insider's as well as the outsider's, would seem to be required: the two should complement, inform and correct each other.

The major difficulty that the Wittgensteinian view encounters is that of demonstrating that religion is a distinct form of life. For it is not entirely clear what a 'form of life' is, and *a fortiori* whether religion is to count as one. Assuming for the sake of the argument that the concept 'form of life' is sufficiently self-explanatory, it is none the less not at all clear whether every form of life, including religion, is altogether autonomous or merely has characteristics which make it more or less distinct from the others. These questions will occupy us more than once in the sequel. For the time being, therefore, I wish to conclude by reiterating what I think has been demonstrated on this occasion, namely, that believing does not seem to be a necessary condition of understanding. Philosophers like Phillips, for example, must surely be wrong in holding a straightforward identity between understanding and believing. I have elsewhere discussed the details of Phillips' claim,[12] and hence will not do so here. But I will point out that traditional fideism itself denies that understanding is a precondition of believing; and the concept of objective understanding – which I think is legitimate – implies the falsity of the view that the latter is a condition, or even invariable concomitant, of the former. And if both these claims are false, then the conjoint claim of identity between believing and understanding cannot possibly be true.

# 7 Religious Language and Truth

There are already many competing accounts of the nature of 'religious language' and its relation to truth. I do not, therefore, think that what is required is yet another new theory about it, and it is not my intention to elaborate one here. Nor is this the place to propose a new general theory of meaning or a method of truth in metaphysics. I do believe, however, that two things may be usefully attempted here: firstly, a brief examination of some of the prevailing views on the subject in order to see whether elements of these can be considered plausible or defensible in the light of conclusions reached so far in this book; and, secondly, to explore if the introduction of an existing philosophical framework not so far applied, not systematically at any rate, to the subject under discussion may help to eliminate certain unnecessary and misleading ways of asking questions and giving answers in relation to so-called religious language.

RELIGIOUS ASSERTIONS AS EITHER MEANINGLESS OR FALSE

I would say that the view that religious assertions are either meaningless or false, as held, (with minor variations in detail) by Ayer,[1] Flew[2] and Martin[3] (among many others), is perhaps the most important. Not only does it represent the essence of sceptical thinking about religion, at least since the days of Hume; it also happens to be the one that most provokes the defensive strategems employed by apologists of religion. What has sometimes been dubbed this 'legacy of Hume' was expressed by Ayer when he said that the religious utterances of the theist were not genuine propositions at all. Flew gave vent to the same line of thinking when he declared that religious assertions, if taken as significant, meet 'death by a thousand qualifications'. Neither of them – nor indeed others of similar views – denied that religious utterances include among them examples which do not set out to state a fact or offer a description of a state of affairs. They only argued that at least some religious utterances must do so, and those of them that do are either incoherent or false. The arguments underlying this conclusion, as indeed their shortcomings, are too well known to merit elucidation here. But it has seemed to many (not all sceptics, by the way) that this line of reasoning put its finger on one essential characteristic of religious discourse: namely, that it does seem to contain what look like assertions or statements of fact. Disagreements related to whether, having correctly analysed the situation so far, the defenders of this view should have gone on to apply to these the kind of verificationism applicable only to straightforward empirical facts, if indeed even to these. But that apart, there does indeed seem to be at least a *prima facie* case for treating certain religious utterances as factual. Belief in the reality of God, heaven, resurrection, reincarnation, redemption, etc, may be just a few examples. The only question worth asking, it seems to me, is 'What kind of fact does religious discourse assert?' This brings us to the second of the views about religious language I wish to consider.

RELIGIOUS ASSERTIONS AS 'SECOND-ORDER FACTS'

John Wisdom argued[4] that the facts stated by religious assertions were not straightforward empirical ones, but rather second-order, what may be called 'metaphysical' facts; and in so far as they are at least purported facts, questions of truth and falsity in relation to them are perfectly in order. On the other hand, though, their truth or falsity cannot be demonstrated empirically, since they are not, typically, first-order empirical propositions. He likens the decision about the truth or falsity of religious beliefs to the final decision in a legal case about what actually happened, after all the evidence – for and against – has been heard. There is a sense in which all that can be stated definitely as true or false has been incorporated in the evidence. Yet, in another sense, or at another level, the lawyers on the opposite sides are still disagreeing about what actually happened – a matter of fact. Religious assertions, likewise, are in some sense claims about what is so; and, according to Wisdom, there are definite procedural limits within which they are to be settled, and the technique for settling them is what he calls one of *connecting and disconnecting*. For if, literally, there were no agreement as to what will settle whether or not a religious claim was correct or true, then such questions would be meaningless.

I consider Wisdom's view to be plausible on two counts. It rightly admits that certain important religious utterances are factual in nature. But, equally importantly in my opinion, he points out that it is misleading to treat all religious assertions as empirical statements, although some of them must be so, obvious examples being historical facts about the birth of Jesus, Mohammed or the Buddha, or those about the geographical location of places of pilgrimage like Jerusalem, Mecca or Benares. Many of the rest, however, are best understood as facts of a different order or kind: they are 'metaphysical facts' for the reason that these are usually affirmed as parts of a metaphysical theory. I feel constrained, however, to disagree with him when he claims, without many qualifications, that there is a definite technique for settling the truth-claims of these through what he calls connecting and disconnecting. There is no doubt that *within* the circle of believers his technique can settle these questions reasonably conclusively: after all, there are usually well-recognised authorities in each religious tradition whose opinions count heavily, e.g. the Pope and/or other ecclesiastical institutions in the case of the Judaic faiths, the Brāhmins and the monks in the case of Hinduism and Buddhism. But are there agreed procedures for settling metaphysical questions from *outside* the religious framework? Can such questions be settled rationally? The variety of attitudes to metaphysics evinced by philosophers since Plato and Aristotle, through Hume and Kant, to Ayer, Quine, Strawson and Davidson would seem to make an affirmative answer implausible. Certainly, in the sense I use 'metaphysical proposition', i.e. as necessarily referring to or presupposing transcendental entities, states, processes, etc, its truth-value, it would seem, cannot be conclusively determined: there appears to be no agreed method available.

RELIGIOUS UTTERANCES AS EXPRESSIONS OF COMMITMENT TO SPECIFIC POLICIES OF BEHAVIOUR

The third of the views about religious language, which at one time received some acclaim, is that put forward by Braithwaite[5] and supported indirectly by Hare (among others). He was in effect accepting the first part of the positivist approach to religious discourse, namely, that this did not consist of genuine propositions.

He took what he regarded as a conativist, as against an emotivist, view of morals and religion.

> The meaning of a religious assertion is given by its use in expressing the asserter's intention to follow a specified policy of behaviour. To say that it is belief in the dogmas of religion which is the cause of the believer's intending to behave as he does is to put the cart before the horse: it is the intention to behave which constitutes what is known as religious conviction.[6]

Not every single religious utterance may be a declaration of policy, but that does not affect the general principle that the meaning of religious utterances is to be found by looking at the believer's commitment to a policy of behaviour. For assertions are made as part of a system which involves the declaration of policy; and, as in the case of scientific hypotheses, the whole system, and not isolated assertions, should be examined for its coherence and truth-value.

Even in this brief sketch of Braithwaite's account, some commendable features should stand out. For example, his emphasis on the commitment to a policy of behaviour as a central feature of religious belief is well placed, although he tends to be rather more dogmatic than he could have reason to be about the priority of behaviour-commitments over belief-commitments. It is by no means evident that saying that a religious person's commitments happen to be what they are because of his belief 'in the dogmas of religion', is 'putting the cart before the horse'. Secondly, his view that religious assertions ought to be assessed for their meaning or truth as a systematic whole or theory, is to the point. But, once again, in taking this view, or at least in its elaboration, he seems to come fairly close to what might look like an extreme relativism. For he says, 'since different people will take different views as to what these fundamental moral principles (of a religion) are, the *typical* meaning of religious assertions will be different for different people'.[7] To say the very least, this would seem to be a strange use of 'typical'.

Braithwaite's main failing, however, lies in his inability to escape the positivist strait-jacket, in spite of his professed aim of giving merely an empiricist's view of the nature of religious belief. Not only does he fail to distinguish between what an assertion means and what the evidence for the believer's commitment happens to be; he positively suggests that the meaning is to be found in the expression of commitment to a policy of behaviour. There is a vast difference between the meaning of an assertion and what role it plays in the life of a believer. Moreover, faced with the question, 'How do we distinguish between two religions which involve the same behaviour-commitments?' or words to that effect, all Braithwaite can say is that the difference lies in the 'stories' told by each: the story is a set of empirical propositions, but in telling it the believer does not assert them as empirical; he merely 'alludes' to them.[8] That believers merely *mention* but do not *refer* to the metaphysical entities, etc. occurring in their belief system runs counter to how the majority of believers themselves understand the situation: God, *Brahman*, *Nirvāna*, etc., are not mere embellishments in a religious story, but real ontological entities to which the system or theory in question commits its adherents.

RELIGIOUS DISCOURSE AS AUTONOMOUS

This brings us, once again, to the discussion of the set of ideas we earlier referred to as Wittgensteinian fideism. The various supporters of this 'school' put forward somewhat different details and strategies, but it is safe to say that there is a central core of ideas to which they all subscribe, some with admittedly greater zeal than others. Nielsen deciphers a certain 'cluster of dark sayings' which together could be said to constitute Wittgensteinian fideism.[9] Since we have already encountered this particular form of fideism, in chapters 1 and 6, here we will only reiterate rather briefly some of its salient features. Its main emphasis, of course, seems to be on the distinctness of religion as a 'form of life', or a 'language game'; and since every form of life is regarded as having its own criteria of intelligibility, reality and rationality, it is claimed that neither science nor philosophy can legitimately evaluate or criticise the claims of religion: all they can do is describe these claims. Forms of life taken as a whole are not amenable to criticism.

I have no doubt that the tenets of fideism should serve to warn us against the hazards of assuming that there is any one central, objective paradigm of rationality – say, that of science – which, therefore, must be applied to all other more or less distinct areas of human activity: standards of rationality must, partly at least, be seen to be governed by accepted practice within the field of activity. Stated in this mild form, it sounds quite plausible. But, if blown into a charter of objective truth, Wittgensteinian fideism turns into a quagmire of half-truths, inconsistencies and absurdities, as witnessed in the religious philosophy of D. Z. Phillips.[10] I have elsewhere examined[11] in some detail the views of Phillips, and will, therefore, here only highlight some of the difficulties he gets into.

For example, he says that, '. . . whereas it makes sense to ask what is truly religious, it makes no sense to ask whether religion as such is true or false'. To claim that the latter question may be unrewarding, given the indeterminacy inherent in the metaphysical nature of many religious propositions, is, to my mind, quite defensible. But that is not what Phillips is saying: he is saying that it makes no sense to *ask* such questions. The regard for every form of life that his brand of fideism entails should have made him take due note of the fact that scepticism is as ancient and venerable a tradition as religious belief. As early as perhaps the sixth century BC, if not earlier, the materialist school of Indian thought, known as Cārvāka, declared that all religious, metaphysical assertions and practices were inventions of the clever to dupe the masses so as to keep the latter under subjugation, or words to that effect. Not only *can* questions about the truth of religion be asked; its falsity has been asserted and reasserted since time immemorial. On what grounds can Phillips, or anyone else, affirm that religion is a form of life but that materialism, hedonism, atheism and scepticism are not?

But perhaps this brings out the problems in drawing the conceptual boundaries of such terms as 'form of life', 'form of language', 'language-game', and other related ones. What constitutes a distinct language? English, French, Sanskrit and Swahili, for example, are recognised as such. Is there also a religious language, an aesthetic language, a language of magic? And how about language-games? How many language-games can be played within a given language? Does each of these languages represent a distinct form of life? Phillips certainly seems to have nothing very helpful to say about these questions, nor, to my knowledge, does any other Wittgensteinian. I do not object to Christianity, Islam or Buddhism being regarded as 'forms of life', provided this is done in a rough-and-ready way. Otherwise, it should be evident to anyone that the extensions of 'the Christian form of life' and, say, 'the scientific form of life', and a few others, are going to overlap.

Given this, the insistence on the autonomy of so-called religious language – certainly evident in Phillips, and implicit in varying degrees in the pronouncements of other Wittgensteinians – would seem to be ill-advised. And if so, then the criteria of truth and falsity in religion need not be exclusively 'internal', as Phillips and others seem to demand. Nor can the autonomy of religious discourse be definitively established with the use of some of Wittgenstein's examples. Let me quote one of these. 'Suppose someone were a believer and said: "I believe in the Last Judgment," and I said: "Well, I'm not so sure. Possibly." You would say that there is an enormous gulf between us. If he said: "There is a German aeroplane overhead", and I said "Possibly. I'm not so sure," you would say we were fairly near.' In answer I will only repeat my comment on this example, made some years ago:

> It is not obvious to me that in the first case there is the 'enormous gulf' that Wittgenstein speaks of. The person who says, 'Well, I'm not so sure. Possibly', is, in traditional terms, an agnostic – one who finds it hard to decide one way or the other. Maybe, he finds it just hard to express himself categorically, in which case he could be a mystic of some sort. To the best of my knowledge, an element of agnosticism has always been integral to mysticism; and who would want to say that there is an immense gulf between the believer and the mystic?[12]

Forms of life may have their own internal logic, but it is not self-evident that these do not yet operate within the framework of an overall rationality expressed as the general 'laws of thought', or 'universal grammar', etc.

RELIGIOUS DISCOURSE AS ANALOGICAL, OR SYMBOLIC

Other analyses of religious language include such famous ones as Aquinas's doctrine of 'analogical predication'[13] (a reasonably well-known and contemporary version of which is Ramsey's 'qualified model' approach)[14] and Tillich's view that religious language is symbolic.[15] I only have time to discuss the former – and that too only briefly. It is my hope that the doctrines that I have discussed will together provide a reasonable commentary on those not discussed here, such as Tillich's, for example. Aquinas took the view that adjectives like 'good', 'loving', etc., when applied to God, are not used either exactly in the same sense that they are when applied to people, nor, on the other hand, are they used with entirely different senses. They are used neither univocally nor equivocally, but *analogically*. When a Christian says that God loves men, he does not mean that he does so in the way that a wife loves her husband or a father loves his son; for God is not a finite, corporeal being. On the other hand, the sense is not entirely different either. As Ramsey would put it, one uses the model of human love to point towards the phenomenon of divine love, but then starts qualifying the model by realising or reiterating that God is infinite, incorporeal, all-loving, all-wise, etc, until, in Ramsey's obnoxious but suggestive phrase, 'the penny drops', and one manages to understand what it means to say that God loves men.

There are two or three features of this account that I find noteworthy. Firstly, by emphasising that 'God-talk' is an analogical extension of talk about humans, it firmly establishes the roots of religious language in ordinary discourse and thus substantially weakens the neo-Wittgensteinian thesis of the autonomy of religious discourse; and perhaps falsifies the claim that there is such a thing as 'religious language', as against the *religious use* of ordinary language. Secondly, it does provide a starting-point in the process of discovering the meaning of religious utterances. And, finally, at least as Aquinas understood it, it points to the metaphysical and, therefore, indeterminate and puzzling nature of many religious assertions. The agnostic, the mystic and the theist positions are shown to be points along a single axis, quite unlike the 'gulf' that Wittgenstein seems to see between one who believes in a day of Last Judgment and one who isn't sure.

THE PROPOSED APPROACH: RELIGIOUS SPEECH-ACTS

My discussion of the prevailing views of 'religious language' has been sketchy and my comments on them highly selective. This is because my intention has not been to present an exhaustive account of these – that is readily available through a great deal of published literature on the subject – but to pick out noteworthy features of these which can then be used as 'pegs' on which to hang the new approach to the subject I propose to introduce. In what immediately follows, I shall list some of these features. I will generally assume that the justification, where necessary, for selecting these has been provided by the preceding discussion, especially in this chapter.

1. While there is a great variety of locutions in religious discourse, some of these are, and must be, fact-stating.
2. Some of these assertions or putative facts are empirical, but

others must be facts of a different order: these could be called 'metaphysical facts'.

3. These metaphysical facts constitute the primary statements of the theory underlying a specific religion.

4. The complete theory consists of these primary statements plus many secondary utterances, including empirical assertions, moral and ritual exhortations, etc.

5. What turns the theory into religion is the background of relevant experiences and the deep, personal commitment of the believer to a specific policy of behaviour (seen by him to be) entailed by the theory.

6. The believer's commitment to a policy of behaviour, or 'way of life', has three broadly distinct aspects: belief-commitments; attitude-commitments and action-commitments.

7. The belief-commitments entail the believer's acceptance of certain transcendental entities, states and processes.

8. Arguably, the attitude-commitments (involving certain kinds of feelings and dispositions, e.g. awe, fear, love, holiness, sacredness, etc.) and the action-commitments (involving prayer, worship and other ritual and moral actions) are consequences of having the particular belief-commitments in question.

9. Religious discourse may be distinct, but is not autonomous: linguistic elements employed in the discourse are largely taken or derived from ordinary discourse, although they are often used for distinct purposes. Consequently, there is no such thing as 'religious language': only religious *uses* of ordinary language.

I take it that these propositions are not only defensible but, in addition, perfectly consistent with the account of religion I have given in the previous chapters. I would further like to claim, especially in view of (9) above, that an adequate analysis of religious discourse requires a broader conceptual framework which allows a distinction to be made between the proposition (or the utterance expressing a proposition) itself and what is being done with it on a given occasion of utterance. Our choice, therefore, it seems to me, should be the terminology of the doctrine of Speech-Acts as enunciated by Austin[16] and elaborated and refined by Searle.[17] This doctrine, as is well-known, takes the view that the same sentence or set of words can on one occasion be used to state a fact, on another to issue a warning, on a third to make a promise, etc. For example, 'I will be there', may be said either simply to inform someone of the fact, or to warn someone against entertaining ideas of mischief, or to reassure the hearer by promising to come. The full meaning, therefore, of 'I will be there' on any given occasion of utterance is discovered not just by noting what the sentence means – although this is important – but, additionally, by taking account of the speaker's intended use of the sentence on that occasion.

These acts – of stating, warning, promising, etc. – are the speech-acts or illocutionary acts performed by the speaker. It should now be evident that the full meaning of religious utterances is found, as in any other area of discourse, by analysing two broadly distinct components: (a) what the words, expressions, etc. mean; and (b) what the speaker means, i.e. what speech-acts are being performed through the use of the linguistic elements (and other non-linguistic devices, such as tone of voice, gestures, etc.) on a given occasion. 'God loves men', or 'Krishna is my lord and master', mean what they do in a religious context not just by virtue of the fact that these expressions have a meaning (in so far as this is non-problematic), but also because the believer has certain intentions and is aware that there are conventions which make it possible for him to express his religious intentions through the use of just those words.

Some typical religious speech-acts may be the following: praising, worshipping, repenting, confessing, forgiving, pleading, thanking, praying, blessing, avowing, affirming, advising, exhorting, pledging, swearing, etc. These expressions (or their equivalents) will, therefore, be typically, though not always, employed to indicate the illocutionary force of the utterance on a given occasion. Examples of some of these may be: 'Praise (or glory) be to the Lord!', 'To thee, Varuna, I offer my oblations!', 'I have sinned against thee, my Lord!', 'I forgive your transgressions, just as the Lord does ours!', 'Give us our daily bread!', 'I thank the ruler of the heavens for keeping my honour!', 'I offer my prayers to Virgin Mary!', or 'Bless thee, my child!' These are examples of religious *speech*-acts, which form only a part of a great variety of other acts, e.g. meditating, fasting, ritual dancing, going on pilgrimages, kneeling, or making the sign of the cross, and a host of others.

These speech-acts, or illocutionary acts, produce effects, either intended or unintended, which may, typically, be these: persuading, encouraging, alarming, converting, confusing, appeasing, exorcising, etc. Such perlocutionary effects form a significant part of religious discourse, and often help to identify the speech-act without having to question the speaker directly as to his intentions. 'Repent before you enter the eternal fires of hell!' spoken by a Billy Graham, leaves no one guessing what perlocutionary effect he may be after. This, however, is a direct threat aimed at conversion; 'God created man in his own image!' spoken with a certain tone of voice and in a particular sort of setting may produce the same or similar results. It is for these reasons that the Wittgensteinian fideist claim that the meaning of an expression is to be found within the appropriate form of life, can be said to be partly justified. But, equally, there is always (or almost always) a conventional reason for the choice of this or that expression for the communication of a certain intention or for the bringing about of a conventional effect; and that is that certain expressions, and not others, mean certain things.

Since these are *acts*, and not expressions, religious illocutionary acts cannot themselves be true or false but only felicitous or infelicitous, happy or unhappy. But where propositions are used to perform these acts, as in 'I tell you that God created heaven and the earth', the proposition involved, namely, 'God created heaven and the earth', may be said to be true or false. But, as remarked earlier, since this is not an empirical proposition nor analytic, its truth-value will be indeterminate. A sceptic will treat it as meaningless or false or both; a believer will insist on its truth, for this may be one of his postulates: and there is no way of conclusively showing who is right. But the indeterminacy of truth-value that a proposition has for reasons of being metaphysical in nature may be lost or transformed when, as sometimes happens, a once-metaphysical proposition eventually renders itself to some form of empirical testing. A case in point may be the Hindu belief in reincarnation. There is little doubt that it originated as a metaphysical belief forming part of the Hindu theory of *Karma*, *Samsāra* and transmigration. But now there are parapsychologists whose professional interest lies in collecting what they regard as evidence for the belief. In principle, therefore, it is possible that in this case either the sceptic or the believer will one day have been shown to be correct.

But what happens to ostensible facts, such as 'God loves men'? Taken in its proper context, i.e. the religious occasion of its utterance, it is very likely to be an act of praise for God or one of reassurance to a believer whose faith has been shaken in some way, or an affirmation of the speaker's commitment to a way of looking at things, although the form of words itself does not indicate whether it is one or the other. The context, however, will generally make it clear. But treated as an assertion, there may be no set of evidence which will prove it true or false: for every occurrence in the world that seems to indicate the loving hand of God, there will be another, or more, which will point in the contrary direction. Its actual truth-value will, therefore, look like being indeterminate for ever. But in a weaker, 'performative' sense[18] of being acceptable by certain specified criteria, it may be called true; for the happiness/unhappiness dimension of illocutionary acts and the truth-falsity dimension of statements cannot, as Austin showed, be kept neatly apart.

To conclude, whatever the difficulties in determining the precise meaning and truth-value of religious utterances, questions about these are not, as a matter of principle, out of place or inadmissible. What does seem to be inadmissible or misleading is the question, 'What is religious language?' What one ought probably to be asking instead is 'What is a religious utterance or speech-act?' And it is unlikely that to this question there can be one uniform or unambiguous answer. For there will be indefinitely many examples of utterances whose form alone would not enable one to place them among religious utterances. There will be examples too where even the study of the context will not remove the uncertainty. This is hardly surprising, for, as I have maintained, 'religious language' shares a great deal with ordinary, 'secular' language. But, *typically*, and in the clearest of cases, one would be able to identify two features characterising a religious speech-act or utterance: (1) the expression used would typically be one taken from the metaphysical-mythological set of statements of a given religion; and (2) the illocutionary force, or speech-act, would usually be indicated by the use of one or another verb listed earlier as expressing religious speech-acts, as in the examples given above. It will be easily seen that these verbs by and large seem to belong to the classes identified by Austin as 'commissives' and 'expositives',[19] although the illocutionary force of many religious utterances may well belong to the other three classes named by him. Where this force is only implicit, the context would usually make it clear which verb may best express the speaker's intention.

The speech-act analysis of 'religious language', it seems to me, makes it unnecessary to labour under the misconception that the whole of religious discourse can, or need, be interpreted in exclusive terms: as statements of fact, of commitments to policies of behaviour, as expressions of emotions and attitudes, as symbolic and/or mythological, as analogical or as 'diabolical' (!). Depending on the context and the occasion of utterance, a piece of discourse may be legitimately seen as being one or more of the above kinds, some hospitable to questions of truth-falsity, others not. The attempt to produce one, uniform account of 'religious language' is misguided and naive in the extreme.

# 8 Science, Magic and Religion

In chapter 5 I took the view that while religion can legitimately be said to have an explanatory function, there are good grounds for not treating it as designed to *control* nature. The plausibility of claims to the contrary will be discussed in the second part of this chapter. In the meantime, I must first consider certain problems that seem to arise if the positive part of my thesis in chapter 5 is accepted, namely, that religious theories do purport to explain. To recapitulate briefly, what I claimed was that while the metaphysical theories underpinning a religion are designed to explain, what they set out to explain is not, typically, the world of ordinary experience or that of common sense, but rather that as appearing in the extraordinary experiences of unique individuals (e.g. the Buddha, Jesus, Mohammed, etc.), peculiar perhaps when first experienced but from then on capable of serving as moulds of perception for others. I also indicated why such experiences, or 'bliks', would inevitably demand explanations; what the model of such explanations might be; and how in most ways the logic of explanation in religion was not unlike that in science, although there were important differences too.

Formidable questions may be seen to arise from the claim that metaphysical theories can be explanatory. It may be argued, against my claim, that no theory can possibly be explanatory unless it satisfies at least two criteria: those of intelligibility and consistency; and metaphysics, it has been widely held in recent years, is straightforwardly devoid of the former and so, indirectly, of the latter as well; consequently it can only offer a pseudo-explanation. Metaphysics, it has been claimed by some, is 'an attempt to say what cannot be said';[1] and, therefore, it is not so much that it is mistaken, but rather that it is confused. Now if metaphysics is, in principle, confused and an attempt to say what cannot be said, then it would follow that metaphysical utterances are logically incoherent: they cannot make sense and only appear to form a theory, whose consistency or explanatory power cannot possibly be put to any test. On the face of it, this is an extremely powerful objection. For the purpose of an explanation is to render more intelligible what was less, or not at all, so; and obviously this cannot be achieved with the help of a theory which is itself a string of words signifying nothing.

That much of what I might call 'academic' metaphysics, as exemplified in its fullness by, say, Hegel and some of the neo-Hegelians, might deserve this wholesale condemnation, is not, to my mind, in dispute. But anyone who today rejects metaphysics in principle is not only belittling the significance of some of the best contributions of great historical figures such as Plato, Aristotle, Spinoza, Leibniz and Kant, but also refusing to take seriously the works of contemporary philosophers such as Strawson, Quine, Davidson and others. It may, however, be said that the charge of incoherence, not to mention obscurity, is meant to apply not to the 'descriptive' metaphysics of the latter set of philosophers mentioned above, but only to the 'revisionary' variety illustrated, in particular, by the transcendental theories embedded in religions, and in certain philosophical systems. My immediate answer to this suggestion would consist of two remarks, neither of which will be defended here, but I have no doubt that they can be defended. First, the distinction between 'descriptive' and 'revisionary' metaphysics is phoney and false; and, second, that obscurity is not a prerogative of metaphysics alone. Besides, saying that one or another kind of metaphysics, or one or another system of it, is obscure is not necessarily showing that it is incoherent. While the claim that a particular system of metaphysics is incoherent can be legitimately entertained if there are grounds for it, there can, in my opinion, be no *a priori* grounds for maintaining that all metaphysics is in principle so.

What, then, can be said about the intelligibility and consistency of the kind of metaphysical theories that form the basis of religions, namely, those theories that incorporate transcendental entities, etc in their cosmology? The discussion in chapter 7 should have brought out the need to distinguish two separate questions that need to be asked in relation to the meaning of any utterance, religious or otherwise: (1) What does the expression mean? and (2) What speech-act is being performed by the speaker through the use of that expression on a given occasion? In relation to question (1), the doctrine of analogical predication (as discussed in chapter 7) shows the way towards determining the meaning of a religious utterance, for the meaning of the expression, more often than not, is an extension of its counterpart in ordinary language. This, however, is only a start, and may indeed leave one with more questions than answers. But, as we also noted, this is not an exclusive feature of religious utterances: an isolated sentence from a theory of physics cannot be understood without some familiarity with the theory itself. So the complete answer to question (1), in so far as this can be had independently of question (2), may be found by placing the expression in its proper place in the theory. However, since the theory in this case will be one entertained and followed in practice by a religious community or individual, a reference to how this community or individual understands it, will be necessary. This brings us to question (2). Since it is the conventions of the community that determine the range of speech-acts that can be performed by the use of a given expression, it would usually be necessary in answering question (2) to be generally aware of such conventions. This awareness, along with a direct or indirect indication of the speaker's intention on a given occasion, should usually prove adequate for an answer to (2). My claim, therefore, is that, in principle, there are identifiable criteria available for establishing the intelligibility of metaphysical utterances forming a religious theory or dogma. Consequently, there do not seem to be grounds of principle for rejecting religious metaphysics as unintelligible, although in practice the criteria cannot be guaranteed in every single instance to lead to answers that may be free from problems, a regrettable but actual state of affairs not just in religion but in any area of discourse whatsoever. In general, however, it seems safe to say that the intelligibility of metaphysical utterances occurring in religious discourse is more or less assured by virtue of the very fact that there are religious communities which successfully communicate through their use.

Now to the question of the consistency of metaphysical theories. It hardly needs to be stated that had there been general, *a priori*, grounds for believing that metaphysical utterances must of necessity lack significance, the question whether they can be internally consistent would not have arisen. Nonsensical statements cannot be said to be either consistent or inconsistent, although if a person habitually makes such statements then he can be said to be more or less consistent in his habit – which, of course, is an altogether different matter. Since we had reason to argue that, while particular metaphysical statements can be said to be unintelligible, there are no *a priori*, or other, general grounds for judging metaphysical utterances *per se* to be senseless, it does nevertheless seem to be an open question at the moment, and an important one, to ask if they are consistent. But it will be evident as soon as the question is raised that it is absurd to answer it *a priori*: there are not, and to my mind, cannot be, *a priori* criteria of consistency which metaphysical theories can be said necessarily to fail to satisfy. The only general answer that can be given, prior to the actual examination of specific theories, will have to be along the lines of what seems to me to be a fairly safe guess: that some may be consistent, others downright inconsistent and quite a few neither wholly one nor the other. I said that this should be a safe guess; and I did so because this seems to be true of theories in general, of which metaphysical ones are a species.

But it may be protested that, surely, religious metaphysical theories hardly deserve the name of theories: they seem by and large to be collections of haphazardly made, *ad hoc* statements. How can God be one and three at the same time, as Christianity believes? How can the Hindu profess on the one hand, that there is one *Brahman*, and, on the other, that there are '330 million gods'? Can Jesus have died and been buried and yet also arisen from the dead? Is it possible consistently to say that there was one individual Buddha, Gautama, who died approximately 2500 years ago, but the 'essence' of the Buddha (*Bodhisattva*) may be reincarnated again and again? These, it will be noticed, are examples – and only a few – taken from the 'sophisticated' world-religions. If one looks at the not-so-sophisticated 'primitive' religions, then, the argument might run, anything like the demand of consistency would be asking for the impossible. Religion, it may be concluded, is not like other theories: more or less consistent internally; consistency would seem to be conspicuous by its absence.

It has to be said that by certain external, say, philosophical standards, religious theories do at least ostensibly present some of the most flagrant paradoxes and puzzles which have troubled not just outsiders but even believers and theologians. If this is not recognised, there will be no explanation either for the admission, by some of the most ardent believers, of the ultimate mystery regarding matters of faith, nor for the rise of the many schools of theology or of 'churches' and sects within a religion. But is this not to be expected in a way? The more general a theory, even inside a given domain, the greater is the possibility of alternative models; and metaphysical theories embedded in religions are, by their very nature, the most general there can be, dealing not just with this or that area of experience but with a particular kind of experience of the world as a whole, and consisting of such questions as the nature of life, death, immortality, rebirth, suffering, the creation and destruction of the world, and so on. Moreover, the same set of original insights by the propounder(s) of a religion are interpreted, or 'perceived', by believers – separated in time and space and partially predetermined by their previous cultural presuppositions – somewhat differently. This fact may attest to the lack of precision or clarity in the formulation of the original insights or to their excessive generality of scope or to the piece-meal nature of the 'revelations': not even Buddhism – to my mind, the most elegant example of a consistent religious metaphysics – could be regarded as an exception. In any case, the function of theology has, among other things, been the attempt to present religious dogma in a consistent and coherent matter. Some theologies have been more successful than others, and in some cases perhaps the task has been hopeless from the start. But on the whole, theories taken together with their attendant theologies do make for greater consistency; and the need to look at things from 'inside' the circle of believers would seem to require taking a metaphysics along with its theology. After all neither quantum theory nor relativity fall together as fully coherent theories – in so far as they do – without taking into account the interpretations of an immense army of gifted scientists working in these areas since the late 1920s, although I admit there may not be a strict parallel here. One final remark to be made here is that paradoxes and anomalies are not in any sense exclusive to religion. After all, science explains heat by identifying it with molecular motion, in the same way as primitive religion identifies rain with spirit and Christianity identifies Jesus with God. If Eddington's 'two tables'[2] can be accommodated within our overall framework, there is no *prima facie* reason why religion cannot reconcile the world of ordinary perception with that of its 'bliks'.

One set of questions that may be uppermost in the minds of critics of metaphysics but which we have not yet discussed directly and will not be doing until the next chapter, is about the empirical content of metaphysical theories incorporated by religions, and other related issues. For in order to be considered genuinely explanatory, a theory not only must be intelligible and consistent but also testable in some way: if there is nothing that would falsify it, or even cast doubt on its validity, then it can only be explanatory in appearance. But assuming for the time being that religious metaphysical theories do satisfy this requirement, even if only in some weak or derivative sense, it would look at this stage that my claim that religious theories do explain, and that they broadly conform to the structures of scientific explanations, although explaining different kinds of experience, is not self-evidently untenable.

Not entirely unexpected support here seems to come from social anthropologists whose theories of religion have been called 'intellectualist'. John Skorupski in his recent work[3] divides social anthropologists of religion and magic broadly into two camps or schools: (1) the 'literalists', who think that 'primitive' people actually and literally believe in the existence of spirits, ghosts, unseen powers of other sorts, and in the efficacy of incantations, spells and charms and of the performance of various ritual acts to produce desired effects, e.g. the killing of an enemy by the ritual act of slaying his effigy, or making rain fall by a ritual dance and/or sacrifice to the 'rain-King'; and (2) the 'symbolists', who suggest that the magical religious practices in question ought to be treated as symbolic acts signifying something other than what meets the eye. Some symbolists see magic and religion as representing psychological facts such as the fears, hopes and anxieties of the relevant peoples and (since the days of Freud) as the acting out of various subconscious neuroses and complexes, e.g. the Oedipus complex. Sociologists among the symbolists, however, notably Durkheim, want these to be understood as 'forms of symbolic statement about the social order'. The literalists – the best-known of whom are Tylor, Frazer, Marrett, etc. – as indeed the symbolists, differ among themselves on matters of detail. But those among the literalists that have been called 'intellectualists' put forward the view that magic and religion ought to be understood in the same terms as science: like the latter, they arose from the need to understand and control nature. The most notable among intellectualists is, of course, Frazer, Horton being regarded as one of the able, contemporary exponents and defenders of intellectualism. It is mainly with Horton's ideas that we will be concerned for a while. But first I would like to make a few general remarks.

In an important sense almost all early anthropological theories of magic and religion – whether literalist or symbolist – tended to be reductionist. As Evans-Pritchard points out,[4] the majority of social scientists who wrote about these subjects had set out to discredit their own religions – mainly Christianity – by showing that religion originated in ignorance and superstition. The symbolists attempted to achieve this by demonstrating that religion was not at all what it seemed to be about: magical and religious practices were either symbolic enactments of deep-seated emotions or else ways of learning and legitimising the social structures, hierarchies and mores of the tribes or societies concerned. Once this was grasped, they hoped, the factual, transcendental claims of religion would have been debunked. The literalists, on the other hand, while accepting the evolutionary basis of the origin of religion, did not deny that the beliefs implicit in magical and religious practices were genuine. But they argued that it was only the ignorance of these early 'savages' which made them entertain those beliefs. Their limited knowledge and faulty reasoning were responsible for the rise of religion; and since modern religions must have originated in similar fashion, the growth of knowledge and, in particular, of science was destined sooner or later to banish the wrong and superstitious beliefs that religion inevitably represented. Early anthropologists were, without exception, committed to the evolutionary approach: the only differences among them related to their *assumptions* about whether primitive peoples' beliefs were the expressions of irrationality or underdeveloped rationality. I use the word 'assumptions' advisedly. For as Evans-Pritchard says,[5] most of the early anthropologists did very little or no field-work and yet attempted to defend their pet doctrines about the origins of religion with the help of highly selective examples of the rites and practices of strange peoples gleaned from unreliable, second-hand accounts. As these theories of religion were avowedly reductionist, their aim would seem to be contrary to my aim of giving a descriptive account of religion, in so far as this is possible. I regard symbolist theories as more overtly reductionist, and will not, therefore, concern myself with these in any important way.

The literalist programme, while it does distinguish between magic and religion, does so, like Tylor, 'rather for convenience of exposition than on grounds of aetiology or validity'.[6] Magic, according to Tylor, has a rational element in what he otherwise regarded as 'this farrago of nonsense'.[7] It postulates impersonal powers in things which can be brought into operation by qualified people for either their own or their clients' ends. It acts on the assumption that effects produced on one thing can be transferred to other things bearing a likeness to it through the 'laws' of contagion and participation, as, for example, the slaying of his effigy causing the death of an enemy. The element of rationality in these beliefs was supposed to show itself in the observations and classifications of similarities on which magical practices are based. But it is none the less mistaken; for the magician wrongly believes that because things are alike, there is a real, mystical link between them. It is 'mistaking an ideal connection for a real one, a subjective one for an objective one'.[8] The difference between magic and religion is largely that the latter replaces the impersonal powers of the former by personal ones: spirits, gods, angels and the like. While not necessarily borne out by subsequent research, Frazer thought that the move from magic to religion marks off a slightly dubious but distinct phase of intellectual development for mankind. People eventually realise, according to him, the futility of magic while still clinging to another illusion: they begin to believe that there are spiritual beings who could help them achieve their objectives – success in hunting or the killing of enemies, etc – if they were propitiated and befriended. The end of the era of illusion, as it were, comes when they realise that the fickle spiritual beings cannot deliver the goods either; and then at last they turn to science, the proper method of achieving control over nature. This brief summary of the relationship between magic, religion and science is only intended to bring out the central feature of intellectualism, namely, that all three have the same objective, although only the last represents the proper means to it, i.e. control over nature. Magic and religion, therefore, can only be seen as bad science: they share the same goal as science, but go about achieving it in wrong and mistaken ways.

The evolutionary approach to the origins of religion underlying the discussion above and, in particular, the distinction between 'primitive' and 'modern' societies that it presupposes, seems to me to be riddled with conceptual problems and confusions. And the dismay is, if anything, intensified by reading that some of these early anthropologists were supposedly philosophers: they obviously did not bring much of their 'modern' critical talents into play when speculating about religion! For a start, their Darwinian sympathies had illegitimately made them assume that the story of the origins of religion must be like that of the origins of species. Consequently, they often allowed themselves the privilege of entertaining opinions about empirical matters without checking the 'facts'. For example, some assumed that the earliest form of religious belief was some kind of animism, only to be told by others that animism was, on the contrary, a highly sophisticated concept only worthy of modern minds.[9] It was not until relatively recently, with the work of contemporary anthropologists like Evans-Pritchard and Horton, that the futility of demonstrating the evolutionary origins of religion was realised, and the task of descriptive anthropology truly begun. The 'primitive–modern' distinction demanded by the early approach was unsatisfactory in many ways. To start with, it had a pejorative connotation, reflecting the self-assumed superiority of European societies, and any others that resembled these sufficiently closely. Secondly, there was an important ambiguity in the use of the word 'primitive': it sometimes presupposed a temporal criterion of demarcation, at other times certain patterns of thinking, an ambiguity which, it seems to me, has not yet been entirely resolved. In its first sense, examples of primitive societies will be those that have been in existence somewhat longer than others, but in its second sense it would clearly have to exclude many examples of societies that are ancient. Egyptian, Indian, Chinese, and Arab societies, while being some of the most ancient, can hardly be said to exemplify 'pre-logical' or 'simple' thinking. One wonders what the principles of classification and the results of their application might have been, had the early anthropologist–explorers been Africans, American Indians, Egyptians or Polynesians!

But despite these reservations, it is not easy to do away altogether with a distinction which, in one form or another, seems to be deemed essential by a whole new discipline. If some such distinction ('primitive–modern', or its equivalent) is indeed necessary for our edification in relation to religion (this remains to be proved, though), I think that Horton's terminology of 'traditional' and 'modern', along with its attendant elucidation of the criteria of distinction, may deserve some discussion. Before we get to that, however, let us note one or two significant features of Horton's intellectualism which set it apart from, say, Frazer's. For a start, religion, and not magic, approximates the character of science more closely: for Horton magic is 'rooted in the lack of a felt distinction between natural and conventional relations between things'.[10] The reliance on magic, therefore, illustrates a feature of traditional, as against modern, thinking. Both Tylor and Frazer tended to take a contrary view: they picked out the apparent fact that magic depended on 'observations' and on the 'laws' – howsoever misconstrued – that seemed to govern relations between things, and so saw a likeness between the magical and the scientific forms of rationality. Real comparability, according to Horton, obtains between religion, on the one hand, and science, the paradigm of modern thinking, on the other. Religion, with its spiritual, transcendental entities, matches scientific theories with their theoretical entities; and each attempts to explain experience in terms of the unexperienced, the empirical in terms of the transcendental. Also both, according to Horton, have the same objective: the explanation, prediction and control of nature. Religion and science, therefore, are similar in structure and function, although only the latter is instrumentally successful. Religion, not magic, is pseudo-science: magic is not even bad science; it is simply nonsense. Horton's overall strategy seems to be the following: 'to differentiate between science and traditional religion as species of the genus *explanatory transcendental hypothesis*; and to differentiate between modern and traditional religion as species of the genus *religion*'.[11]

For this strategy to work, Horton needs to draw an exhaustive inventory of contrasts, on the one hand, between traditional religious thought and modern science, and, on the other, between traditional and modern religion. What he seems to end up doing, however, is make the latter distinction merely by giving examples of each. By 'traditional religion' is meant, for example, tribal African religions; and by 'modern religion' world-religions such as Christianity, Islam, Buddhism and, presumably, Hinduism. By the further steps of selecting Christianity as the paradigm of modern religions (on grounds not clearly spelt out, to the best of my knowledge), and of stressing the modernity of modern Christianity and modern science, he conflates the two sets of contrasts in his strategy into a single one: that between 'traditional' and 'modern' thought. Some of his moves seem clearly to be arbitrary and some of his assumptions questionable, to say the very least. But it is still, in my opinion, important to look at the contrasts.

Horton follows other intellectualists in claiming that the difference between traditional and modern thought lies not in their content but in attitudes; and the five attitudes that mark it off are the following:[12]

1. Traditional thought is *unreflective*, i.e. it does not concern itself with epistemological and methodological issues arising out of its theories about the world.

2. Traditional thought is *unsystematic*, in the sense that the traditional thinker or cosmologist does not self-consciously present

his beliefs as a systematic, unified body, although this can be done. *More importantly, there is no attempt at, or even thought of, putting this 'body' of beliefs to any kind of experimental or empirical test.*

3. While modern thought is characterised by the twin motives of explanation and prediction, traditional thought has mixed motives; that is to say, it has other needs and goals, such as emotional and aesthetic ones.

4. Traditional thought does not, by and large, have the counterpart of specialists in theory-making or intellectuals, as witnessed in scientific activity.

5. Traditional thought has a protective, uncritical attitude to established beliefs and concepts. Or, to put it in Weberian terms, it gains its authority from 'piety for what actually, allegedly or presumably has always existed'. Scientific thought, on the other hand, is legitimised by its power to cope with the relevant facts.

Although I do not have the space to show this in any detail, I feel that each of these contrasts is either insufficiently grounded or positively false. Items 3, 4, and 5 look especially vulnerable: it is by no means evident that emotional and aesthetic goals do not enter into scientific thought; it is possible that there may be more or less specialised intellectuals in traditional societies, although the structure of such societies does not on the whole require elaborate specialisation; and if Kuhn is right, scientific thought may not differ significantly from traditional thought in the legitimisation of its beliefs. We shall be discussing this last point, and the related one in item 2 above, in somewhat greater detail in the next chapter. In the meantime, I would say that, like certain other contrasts, the one between traditional and modern thought (as indeed between traditional and modern religion) is only useful if it is not overdone. There is indeed a difference of degrees: I myself took the view in chapter 5 that, as we move from traditional to modern religions, the aim of control over nature seems gradually to give way to that of understanding and explanation only. But a sharp distinction, I suspect, would be untenable.

Let me now conclude by summing up my agreements and disagreements with Horton. My main disagreement – apart from those relating to his strategy leading to the contrast between traditional and modern thought, and to the apparent sharpness of the contrast itself – is that I find it hard to see religious theories (whether traditional or modern) as primarily motivated by the desire to control nature. In chapter 5 examples were given to show that even traditional societies distinguished between instrumental action proper, e.g. hunting, farming and killing, on the one hand, and ritual performances on the other, like dancing before getting ready to hunt, blessing the land before starting ploughing and slaying effigies of enemies, etc. The structure of scientific and religious thinking may be similar, but it is not identical, as Horton and the other intellectualists seem to suggest. Not only do I doubt the validity of control as a function of religious thought, I also dispute that the two types of theories – religious and scientific – explain the same thing, namely, the world of ordinary experience. I am not sure if I want to go as far as claiming, with Bergson, that the two types of activity – religious and scientific – are rooted in two different sources, the former in instinct and intuition, the latter in the intellect and reason.[13] But I do want to maintain that the experiences or 'perceptions' that they seek to explain are different in the two cases.

Where I whole-heartedly agree with Horton is in holding that religion and science are species of the genus *explanatory transcendental theories*. It is precisely for this reason that I have argued that transcendental metaphysics is an essential part of the concept of religion. If metaphysics is the core of religion, as I believe it is, it could be said that it is the 'torch-bearer' of science. If this seems to blur distinctions between metaphysics, science and religion, then I must confess that the blurring is quite intentional and, I hope, justified. Some boundaries have been too rigidly drawn in recent philosophy; and a little flexibility could be salutary.

# 9 The Rejection of Religious Belief

In the preceding chapters I have taken certain positions whose conjoint implications must now be assessed. While I have advocated the need for examining not only what expressions mean but also what speech-act is being performed in the use of a given expression on a given occasion of utterance – the two sets of considerations jointly determining its full meaning – I have clearly taken the view that some religious utterances look like and are meant to be assertions. Since some of these assert what I called 'metaphysical facts', the question that must be asked is: 'How do we verify the truth or falsity of metaphysical assertions?' The problem is that since they typically refer to certain items beyond experience, and to which are predicated expressions which at best have an analogical relationship to acts of predication in ordinary discourse, there would seem to be no easily identifiable method of verification. The standard method relating to empirical truths does not seem to be applicable. When John loves Mary, I can talk to John and watch his behaviour; but when the assertion is 'God loves men', one cannot talk to God and ask him if this is true. When it comes to watching his 'behaviour', since the scope of the claim is virtually universal, there would, it seems, be as many bits of evidence supporting as opposing it. Some would wish to state the problem in starker terms: there is no such thing as God, and this failure of reference must make the assertion either false or void. Flew's conclusion from the parable of the invisible gardener is a case in point: if the supposition makes no identifiable difference to what is or could be the case empirically, then it is either gratuitous or false. It is easy to generalise from such instances and claim that it looks as though no possible state of affairs in the world could make any difference to the religious person's beliefs; and if this is so, then the believer's behaviour is irrational, superstitious, unjustified.

To a fideist, this sort of objection presents no serious threat: he does not claim that religious belief is rational; the whole point of the contrast between faith and reason is that matters of faith ought not to be judged by rational, and, therefore, 'external' criteria. The claim of complete autonomy for religious belief and discourse is a short step from here. Philosophical and scientific criticism or 'evaluation' of religious matters is fundamentally misguided. Some fideists, grudgingly it seems, allow philosophy a minor, worse than an 'underlabourer's', role: it can analyse and clarify religious concepts; but what it cannot, must not, do is pass judgment on the truth-falsity of religious claims. Since I have argued for the rejection of fideism, although conceding that questions of meaning in religion do require reference to the community or tradition of believers, it seems that I must have recourse to one of two alternatives. I must either deny that religious belief goes on regardless of what happens in the world, or concede that religion is irrational – not just non-rational, as fideism maintains – and superstitious. Since I have also already taken, and defended, the position that, although there are important differences, religious theories have a rational structure and function, it follows that I really have no choice but to defend, if I can, the first of the alternatives: that is, to deny that religious belief is immune to empirical facts, philosophical reasoning and scientific discoveries. Fortunately, I think that this can be done, as the sequel will show.

The discussion above started with the question of the truth-falsity and method of verification of particular religious utterances. But, as I indicated in chapter 7, I agree with the view that propositions which form part of a theory have to be judged for their truth-falsity as a whole, i.e. as a theory. Especially since my position is that religious systems, apart from anything else, are explanatory theories, they must satisfy some criteria of testability, otherwise one would never be able to tell if they actually succeed in explaining what they set out to explain. A theory which explains everything cannot be said to explain anything at all: its explanatory appearance must be deceptive. In other words, the assumption of its truth must be inconsistent with *some* state of affairs; and if any of these states of affairs actually obtains, then, in principle, the theory must be deemed to be false, or at least suspect. If a theory is not falsifiable, then according to Popper, it is not a genuine, explanatory, theory, but plain metaphysics: falsifiability, for Popper, is the criterion of demarcation between scientific and metaphysical theories.[1] Since I have been consistently arguing that religious theories are metaphysical, it would look as though, if Popper is right, they cannot be genuinely explanatory. But I have also been maintaining that they are so. Consequently, I must be committed to the view that Popper is in fact wrong; and this indeed is the case. I have elsewhere discussed my reasons for rejecting Popper's doctrine,[2] and would, therefore, not go into them here. I will, however, point out that there are alternatives to Popper's account of scientific method: the inductivist and the Kuhnian, for example. In addition, I would here argue that it is possible for a theory to be metaphysical and yet explanatory, as I maintain religious theories are. I do, however, hold that explanatory theories must satisfy some requirement of testability, even if it is only in a relatively weak sense of the term (as opposed to the stronger demands of testability made on scientific theories). I interpret this weak criterion of testability as entailing, in the present case, the denial of the view that religious belief is immune to empirical facts, philosophical reasoning and scientific discoveries. Before I proceed with this denial, however, I consider it important to explore yet another route through which one may arrive at this task, namely, the need to show that religious belief does not, as a matter of fact, go on regardless of anything else.

Tylor asked, naturally in relation to traditional religious and magical doctrines, why people went on believing them, when it should have been apparent to anyone in due course that they did not work. This, it will be seen, is making the same assumption that we have encountered earlier, namely, that religious beliefs go on regardless of facts. His answers, therefore, should be of interest. According to Tylor, this phenomenon can be explained by the following set of reasons:[3] first, the predictions made on the basis of these doctrines were vague and indefinite, so that they could not easily be falsified. Also, some of these were of a self-fulfilling nature. Here he was presumably referring to predictions which were more or less of the form: 'if you perform such and such a rite, you will feel better, stronger, etc.' Then again, in such societies success always made a greater impact than failure. More importantly, however, the rites and rituals often accompanied proper instrumental action, such as sowing seeds for crops, thus ensuring that the desired results were achieved. Many of these rites were performed to bring about events which would have occurred anyway, for example, the onset of seasons, etc. If there was a failure, however, it could always be blamed on some impropriety or omission in the performance of the rites. And, finally, the supposition of these people that the results were not entirely governed by the rite: there were always other factors too. In cases of failure, therefore, one could always think of other rites, or other magical or spiritual agencies as having intervened. These factors together ensured the unfalsifiability of these beliefs.

To students of the history of science, many of these factors would appear familiar: 'saving the appearances' by having recourse to *ad hoc*, auxiliary hypotheses is a persistently recurring practice in the history of scientific thought, the most conspicuously notorious example being the attempt to retain the geocentric theory of Ptolemy. Whenever a new observation tended to conflict with the theory, yet another 'epicycle' was added, with the result that the theory eventually became so cumbersome as to be virtually unworkable; and it was its inelegance, it may be noted, that led to its subsequent replacement by the Copernican theory. Resistance to new doctrines and the conservative attitude of persistence with established beliefs, does not seem to be an exclusive feature of 'primitive' thought. We will return to this theme later. In the meantime, it should be noted that scepticism about prevailing ideas is not altogether an unknown phenomenon in these societies: people often were sceptical towards some medicine men as opposed to others, and towards some medicines as opposed to others. Skorupski quotes the following passage from an anthropologist's report: 'Vansina recalls affectionately three very independent thinkers he encountered among the Bushong, who liked to expound their personal philosophies to him. One old man had come to the conclusion that there was no reality, that all experience is a shifting illusion. The second had developed a numerological type of metaphysics, and the last had evolved a cosmological scheme of great complexity which no-one understood but himself.'[4] Such instances of scepticism cast doubt on Tylor's assumption that the beliefs of these peoples went on regardless of anything: evidently, the conflict between theory and fact, dogma and speculation was registered. Perhaps Tylor's complaint is that there was no rejection, not a widespread one anyway. But then, there are good reasons why a widespread, overt rejection is not to be expected. The question that one should ask is: how would Tylor have recognised rejection of belief if it did occur but not on a large scale, and not in any obvious, explicit way? I would like to call this difficulty the 'opacity' of the phenomenon of rejection, but will not elaborate on it until a little later.

Let us now come to the main issue that we have postponed time and again: the rejection of religious belief. The supposition that religious beliefs are held irrespective of facts, philosophical reasoning and scientific findings will only be true if such beliefs are never discarded. But this, I maintain, is false. Rejection occurs in three broadly distinct patterns: (1) that of an entire religion by an identifiable group of individuals, who may or may not go on to adopt another religion; (2) that of a particular dogma or item of faith of one religion by an identifiable group; and (3) that of an entire religion (or important parts of it) by an individual. One clear example of the first kind that comes to mind is the public, *en masse* rejection of Hinduism by the late Dr Ambedkar (a cabinet colleague of former Prime Minister Nehru) and his followers. Dr Ambedkar was a member of one of the 'untouchable' castes, who led his followers to the rejection of Hinduism, and the adoption of Buddhism, because he could no longer live with the Hindu belief and practice of caste, especially the obnoxious one of 'untouchability'. This was undoubtedly a form of political protest, but the crucial issue is that this was done because he and his followers could no longer accept the implications of an important tenet of Hinduism. Another example of this kind could be the well-known phenomenon of youths in Christian countries taking to oriental religious cults of various sorts. To argue, as some presumably would wish to do, that these are not really examples of rejection but only of youthful rebellion, would seem to me to be an instance of 'saving the appearances' in reverse.

Rejection of the second kind is illustrated by such phenomena as the widespread disregard by Catholics of the Pope's encyclical on artificial methods of contraception: the consciences of the Catholics concerned could no longer accept the papal line in the face of the new realities of the world. In case this is seen as not really being a rejection of primary doctrine, one could cite the recent example of a group of leading theologians denying the dogma of the literal resurrection of Jesus Christ,[5] quite definitely a central plank in traditional Christian doctrine. The denial by many modern Hindus of the validity of a hereditary caste-system – itself a degenerate form of the ancient Vedic system of the four classes – while not rejecting the rest of Hinduism itself, should also count as an instance. I would have thought that rejection of this sort, even though it is sometimes euphemistically called a mere 'demythologising' of dogma, is quite common in the context of virtually any religion.

The third kind of rejection – in which an individual, once a believer, can no longer subscribe to the tenets of his former faith, or when he can no longer look at things from a religious point of view – is equally common, although only a few instances, involving celebrities of one sort or another, come to be widely known. One informal way of indicating the extent of this kind of rejection is that virtually every educated individual personally knows a few people who have turned non-religious, or 'become atheists', to put it in terms commonly employed to designate rejection in the Judaeo-Christian parts of the world, although in my own terminology atheism is not necessarily the same thing as irreligiosity. The fact that instances of such rejection are not widely heard of or recorded is, to my mind, merely evidence for what I have called the opacity of the phenomenon of rejection. But, once again, more on that later.

At this point we ought to look at one implication of an extreme form of neo-Wittgensteinian fideism, best (or is it 'worst'?) illustrated, once again, by D. Z. Phillips. According to him, and certain others, one's religious beliefs are the very frameworks of one's judgment of everything else: they are the 'absolutes' which provide the criteria of assessment of the truth–falsity, value–disvalue of other beliefs and attitudes; and cannot, therefore, themselves be the objects of scrutiny and possible rejection. This extreme position leads Phillips to taking (at least) two indefensible positions: first, that non-religious facts and theories do not, or should not, have any bearing on one's religious beliefs; and, second, his identification of believing and understanding. As for the first of these claims, its falsity, I believe, is demonstrated by the instances of rejection discussed above, for there seems not the slightest doubt that these are 'triggered off', or, as I will show later, belief is gradually 'corroded' by extra-religious factors. Here the second of his theses is brought in to argue that cases of rejection are not really so, for if someone does seem to reject his faith, he could not have been a believer in the first place. If the believer had understood the nature and significance of his belief, he could not possibly have rejected it. As Phillips might put it: 'To understand "God" is to love him!' and, therefore, to have faith in him. Since some at least of the examples of rejection and rebellion have been people of great intelligence, sympathy and integrity, Phillips is led by his thesis into the absurdity of insinuating naivety or stupidity on their part. But this still does not make him give up his 'identity thesis'. Replying to MacIntyre's criticism that the identification of believing and understanding makes it impossible to give an intelligible account of the rejection of religious belief, Phillips still, doggedly, says: 'Clearly some kind of modification of my (autonomy) thesis is called for, I agree. But what is not called for is a denial of the identification of belief and understanding in religion.' As I have said elsewhere,[6] nothing but such a denial would seem to be called for. I have tried to show the falsity of this identification in some detail in chapter 6. So I will say no more here on that subject, and simply conclude that it does not seem to be the case that 'religious belief goes on regardless . . .' etc.

Those who may have been convinced by my argument that rejection of belief is a fact – demonstrating the falsity of the claim that metaphysical, and, in particular, religious, theories are indifferent to what happens in the world – may, however, still feel inclined to wonder why, in that case, religions are not discarded (as scientific theories are), collectively and self-consciously. Here at least two things need to be said. First, I have only argued that there is a *similarity* of structure and function between religious and scientific theories. I have not claimed – indeed, positively rejected – *identity* between the two: I have, for example, denied that religious theories share the goal of prediction and control of nature. It follows then that even if strict falsifiability did govern scientific practice – which is not the case – it need not necessarily determine religious practice. Since religious theories, on my account, merely share the broad explanatory function of scientific theories, all that can be reasonably expected is that the former satisfy *some*, possibly weaker, criterion of testability; and the fact of rejection seems to me to indicate that such is the case. More to the point, however, is the fact that I regard Kuhn's account of paradigm-shift as a closer approximation to scientific practice.[7] Scientific theories are seldom discarded dramatically, 'overnight', as it were, just because some set of observations or experiments seems to falsify their predictions. The reluctance of scientists to drop established theories is not markedly less than that of 'primitive' religious communities. All of Tylor's observations and explanations of how and why traditional societies go on believing what they must themselves somehow see as manifestly false, can be said to apply in varying degrees to the practice of scientific communities; *although this comparison must not be overdone*. Given this, what may appear to be surprising is that religion is rejected at all, not why this is not done in more dramatic ways, or on more massive scales.

Nor is this 'reluctance' a mere psychological quirk, or a piece of political prudence. *Logically*, too, this is as it should be. When there is a theory comprising a large number of statements, no recalcitrant fact could conclusively establish the falsity of any particular one of these: it could point to the possible falsity of one or another of several possible candidates. Equally, the recalcitrant 'fact' itself could be construed as a consequence of the experiment being conducted imperfectly. If the defectiveness of the experimental set-up could not be demonstrated, and a scientist was determined to defend a particular part of the theory against apparently falsifying evidence, he could always do so by modifying the rest of the theory, by introducing an auxiliary hypothesis. The falsification of a well-formed theory is more an exception than the rule; and this is primarily because theory is 'underdetermined' by experience – actual as well as possible. I am reminded of a story that demonstrates tellingly, I think, the use of auxiliary hypotheses in a religious context. A rural Hindu who claimed to be able to produce rain with the aid of a local god who 'possessed' him on ritual occasions, said, after the failure of one of these rites to produce rain: 'Did you not see the great big clouds to the east of our village yesterday? *My* god, you see, was bringing the cloud-burst right here, but, the god of the village next-door pinched it for them!' The possibility of this kind of explaining away of potentially falsifying experience is inherent in the logic of theories; and not only religious people exploit it.

Having defended the empirical relevance of religious theories and their explanatory character, I now turn to giving a positive account of the process of rejection as well as of retention of religious belief. While the reluctance and slowness to reject theories characterises scientific as well as religious practice, there is no doubt that this is much more pronounced in the latter; and there are obvious reasons for this. Scientists may get attached to their pet theories but science is meant to be a detached search for 'objective' truth; it is not, typically, an emotional response to the world: its idiom is decidedly impersonal. Religion, on the other hand, involves one's emotions, attitudes, ideology and values – almost all that is personal and subjective in one's life. This is why 'deep, personal commitment' is an integral part of religion, as I see it. This factor of personal commitment should explain – if explanation is needed – why the rejection of religious belief would be relatively rare; and a slow, painful process when it does occur. For religious people, their beliefs are not tentative working hypotheses to be discarded as soon as a better one comes along. As I explained in chapter 5, to call religious theories explanatory in function is not to say that for believers there is anything provisional about it: for them it is not awaiting verification or falsification. In accepting the beliefs as their own, they tacitly accept their truth and commit themselves wholeheartedly to a policy of behaviour – to lead their life in certain ways. Their commitment precludes deliberate questioning of their postulates, although no reflective person can avoid doing so altogether. Religious beliefs are not, in my opinion, 'absolutes', but nor, on the other hand, are they mere opinions. They do happen to constitute the believer's fundamental conceptual framework. But even conceptual frameworks can change, just as paradigms in science change.

The discussion of commitment brings us to the spelling out of the opacity of rejection. Since commitment is integral to religious belief, one major form that rejection takes is the gradual loss of commitment: the believer no longer has any use for the 'picture', as Wittgensteinians would want to put it. This phenomenon presents a problem of identification. While belief in the theory, or operative parts of the doctrine or metaphysics of one's religion, and, therefore, the personal commitment, may have been gradually corroded, this need not be very apparent; and for a very good reason. Religion in the sense of culture, signifying certain values and a certain manner of expressing them – that is not easily rejected. Unless the loss of personal commitment is of such intensity that the person concerned cannot bear to live in his culture any longer – a very rare event – he may, for all appearances, continue to behave in former ways. The conviction and the commitment may be gone, but old habits and the fear of adopting strange cultures or idioms may ensure that the former believer continues to behave very much as he used to. This covert form of rejection is what the Church and other religious authorities seem mainly to be complaining about in their talk of the 'decline of faith'. For obvious reasons, this form of rejection is not easily detected: its opacity almost makes it go unrecognised. But when this factor is taken into account, rejection may not appear to be as rare an event as some claim it to be.

If my account of the fact of rejection is correct, I need to explain what causes it. I suggest that, while admittedly the religious believer does not set out consciously to subject his beliefs to possible refutation, a kind of 'subterranean testing' goes on inside every believer. Whether he likes it or not, and however much he may in some ways wish to resist it, a reflective believer is always susceptible to what goes on around him. New experiences, significant events, new ideologies, philosophical criticism, scientific discoveries – all make an impact on him. While his commitment to his religious beliefs is the most important for him, he must, as a socially alive and responsible creature, have other commitments as well. As long as his beliefs do not conflict with the legitimate demands of, say, science, philosophy, ideology and common sense, or as long as his inventiveness manages to equip him with suitable auxiliary hypotheses accommodating the conflict, he may continue in his faith. But every single failure of accommodation, or every experience of severe problems in effecting this accommodation leaves its mark. As the frequency and intensity of these increases, the threshold of rejection may be reached. The deep commitment makes it inevitable that the believer would find this process of 'corrosion' painful, hard to live with. When the conflict and the pain experienced reach a certain 'boiling point', the believer rebels and rejects. But since this involves rejecting all that was of the maximum personal significance and worth in his life, the very framework that made him lead his particular way of life, it is unlikely that for a genuinely committed believer rejection would be anything but a shattering experience. Since believing – when it is a conscious choice – involves what in existentialist terminology may be called 'fear and trembling', loss of belief may, not unnaturally, cause a feeling of futility and emptiness. The acquisition as well as the loss of faith are moments of great personal significance in one's life. To conclude: if it is at all helpful to speak in this way, the dialectic of religious belief consists not of straightforward conjectures and refutations, but rather of the triad of conjecture (intuition, speculation, *et al.*), commitment and criticism. It originates in theorising triggered off by experience, is stabilised by commitment, nurtured by reflection, criticism and doubt; and it is the last of these that leads, when it does, to rejection.

# 10 Religion and Rational Choice

Throughout the previous chapters I have consistently defended the position that there is a similarity of structure and function between religious and scientific theories, although rejecting identity between them. If this is correct, then the processes governing choice in the two domains ought to be comparable. Since it is generally assumed that the choice between rival scientific theories, and also the decision as to which part of a given theory is to be abandoned in the face of recalcitrant facts, is governed by rational criteria, one would be entitled to expect that this is also the case in the context of religious beliefs. In previous chapters, especially chapter 9, an attempt was made to show that there is indeed a 'logic' involved in the adoption (when this is a conscious choice), retention and rejection of religious belief. I argued that this logic, 'dialectic', as I called it, consists of conjecture, commitment and criticism, steps which ought to be recognised as rational. 'Purists' who might wish to delimit the scope of 'rational' to a process which confines itself to one of strict logical deductions and wherein emotional, aesthetic, moral and prudential considerations play no part, ought to be reminded that such unadulterated reasoning only operates in formal logic and mathematics, if indeed even in these. I accept Kuhn's account of scientific practice[1] to the extent that it truly depicts the role of non-rational factors – emotional, aesthetic, pragmatic etc – in the *actual* rejection and retention of scientific theories and their modification and sophistication, although the *intention* of scientists may well be to operate on the Popperian model of straightforward conjectures and refutations, strictly determined by deductive procedures. Perhaps this is not the appropriate place for it, but I cannot help saying that the controversy among philosophers of science relating to whether inductivism, Popper *or* Kuhn gives *the* correct account of scientific activity, is misplaced and misleading in so far as it sees or portrays them as strict alternatives. Each of them, it seems to me, captures certain features of historical and actual scientific practice, not unlike the picture in philosophy of religion where emotivists, conativists, symbolists, cognitivists and fideists all pick out certain characteristic features of religious discourse and activity but then, wrongly, in my opinion, claim one or another of these to be definitive and exclusive. Rationality as evidenced by any non-formal, 'living' domain of human activity never presents a simple, pure structure. It does, and must, however, display a core which we conveniently designate 'common sense', 'laws of thought', etc; and appearances notwithstanding, religion, it seems to me, is no exception to this rule.

Much of what I have said in the previous chapters should, I hope, have demonstrated the truth of this contention in different ways. Here I must face a somewhat more specific issue. Is there anything resembling scientific theory-change in religion? If so, is this a rational process; and if not, why not? Here one or two things must be stated candidly. Religion is not typically regarded as an area where anything resembling a straightforward 'paradigm-shift' could be said to occur. There are examples of religion which were once practised but which are now dead, and of those which now have only a small following (Zoroastrianism, for example), but these are seen as illustrating historical facts such as conquest, conversion, persecution or simply the extinction of an identifiable population group. No one would want to suggest that these religions were deliberately abandoned because of their inadequacy or inability to cope with newly discovered facts or experimental data. Their demise is not self-evidently like the abandonment, on largely rational grounds, of geocentrism, the phlogiston theory, the corpuscular theory of light or of Newtonian mechanics. Quite the contrary. While individuals or small groups of them may have rejected particular faiths, the main religions – Hinduism, Buddhism, Judaism, Christianity, Islam – seem to be going on very much as they did centuries ago, although reinterpretations and modifications of doctrine and ritual have taken place in varying degrees. This fact cannot be glossed over, although it is easy to exaggerate its significance.

Examples of the broad patterns of rejection of religious belief were given in the last chapter to show that these display a basically rational logic. It was also argued that there is one particular form of rejection which is not easy to detect, but is substantial all the same, namely, the loss of commitment. This loss of commitment, often arising out of the loss of conviction in the rationality or adequacy of one's beliefs, sometimes does lead an individual to the adoption of another faith considered more satisfying – intellectually and otherwise. But there is another, rather important, fact too. Arguably, Buddhism may be said to have the same, or similar, relation to Hinduism, or Christianity and Islam to Judaism, as, say, relativity theory and quantum mechanics to Newtonian physics. It is true that the rise of Buddhism did not lead to the demise of Hinduism: quite the reverse in fact, if one takes into account the virtual disappearance of Buddhism from India itself. Nor did Christianity and Islam destroy Judaism, even though attempts were continually made, not often through an appeal to principles of rationality! It should be recalled that modern physics has not banished Newtonian theory: it merely takes the view that the latter has a narrower, certainly different, domain of application. Similarly, Buddhism was seen by some, historically, as a better formulation of Hindu insights; and Christianity and Islam were seen by their followers as more universal and 'truer' expressions of certain Judaic beliefs. The point I am trying to make here is that it is possible to argue that the growth and development of religions may have a pattern broadly similar to that of scientific theories and ideas – namely, a core of rational considerations accompanied by varying degrees of emotional, aesthetic, political and prudential prejudices and predilections.

Having said this, however, I do want to return to the position that on the whole religion does not noticeably exemplify the process of growth and theory-change in science. Nor is this surprising. For a start, it is more directly and intimately rooted in the believer's emotional response to the world than science is or could be. Indeed, in the latter case, there should, ideally, be no emotion involved; and one is surprised when one encounters it in scientific practice. Moreover, religion has, as we noted in the last chapter, a large cultural dimension which is not easily shed. Most people are products of one or another religious culture whose values, attitudes and ideologies they grow up with, and which only a few have the need, ability or willingness to grow out of. Science has not until recently, if indeed at any time, been a culture: it has been a corpus of knowledge, and so, almost by definition, dictated the adoption of ideas which seemed more closely to approximate truth. Here one must note a striking contrast between the scientific and the religious approaches. Science has by and large assumed that there was a body of truths which it was the business of the scientific enterprise to discover. Religion, on the other hand, has on the whole tended to believe that this body of truths was already discovered and enshrined in the theory and practice of this or that particular religion. Given this, it is hardly surprising that practitioners of a religion do not go out of their way to subject their beliefs to deliberate refutation and stay ever-ready to embrace new and rationally more satisfying theories. Each religious system assumes its own truth and is either altogether inhospitable to others or else reluctantly prepared to make minor amendments to its tenets, if this is found absolutely necessary in the face of disclosures made by other religious doctrines, by science or by philosophy, and the like.

It may be said that even on this particular count there is not so sharp a contrast between religion and science as one might imagine. In practice even scientists proceed by accepting their theories as true, albeit only provisionally, and then subjecting them to tests in order to determine whether they might not be false after all. The assumption of the truth of a theory is a practice, it may be urged, which is not exclusive to religion. But, on the other hand, while this may in science be only a pedagogical device, in religion there is nothing merely methodological about it. Unlike science, religion does not proceed on the assumption that its tenets are only true until proved false: the belief-system is genuinely regarded as reflecting the nature of reality itself. This point is noteworthy, for if true, as I believe it is, then religious practice may be said to rest on *realist* premises, whether or not this has been stated or realised by believers, historically. *Relativist* accounts of religious belief, therefore, face a serious handicap, in my opinion: religions themselves have not, typically, embraced relativism. They have not generally countenanced the Protagorean maxim that man is the measure of all things, even though many of their conceptions can be seen to be highly anthropomorphic.

This introduction of 'realism' and 'relativism' into our discussion is not gratuitous, as will be evident later. But an awful lot of dust can be raised unnecessarily unless care is taken to spell out as clearly as possible the senses of these terms and the various kinds of realism and relativism.[2] To start with, there is a contrast between them in the context of the determination of what there is. In this context, a realist is one who believes that there is a reality quite independent of human perception and conception; a relativist denies this and insists that what exists is, and must be, relative to human perception, conception, theories or frameworks. These are examples of *ontologi-*

*cal* realism and relativism. Related to, and sometimes buttressing, these are *semantic* realism and relativism. The semantic variety is a somewhat late arrival on the philosophical landscape, at least in its explicit form, and has been the focus of interest in much contemporary philosophy, although its reverberations have already reached contemporary social science. Semantic realism takes the view that the meaning of a sentence is determined by discovering its 'assertability conditions', i.e. by finding out what actual or possible states of affairs would warrant or justify its assertion. I cannot legitimately assert, 'There is a bull in the field', unless there *is* a bull in the field; for if I were allowed to make the assertion in the absence of a bull, I might as well have the authority to assert 'There are unicorns in the field', or 'There are androids playing football on the field'. And if so, there would seem to be no detectable difference between the senses of the three sentences. For an assertion to have sense, there must be some conditions which, when they obtain, entitle me to make it; and when they do not, I can no longer do so. Semantic relativism, on the other hand, may reject this analysis of meaning: meaning is not determined by the assertability conditions of a sentence but by its place in a theory or belief-system. Alternatively, the relativist position may accept that meaning is determined by assertability conditions, but then go on to insist that these conditions are only specifiable within the framework of a theory. People do not make assertions, promises, pledges, etc, except within the framework of a theory, culture or form of life. Consequently, assertability conditions, and thus, meaning, cannot be determined except by looking at what a sentence does in the given theory or form of life. Realism and relativism here are theories of meaning, and, while they may, they need not necessarily be espoused in support of their ontological counterparts. Quite distinct from the two kinds of relativism mentioned above, there may be a third, of a very different kind, which could be called 'cultural', or 'descriptive'. Cultural relativism is not a philosophical doctrine about either reality or meaning: it may simply be a descriptive claim that societies, cultures, forms of life, etc, do, as a matter of fact, differ in their judgment of what there is, and of how we should behave and live. Cultural relativism may sometimes be brought in to support either ontological or semantic relativism, usually the former. But since it is not itself a philosophical thesis, its truth or falsity does not automatically guarantee that of philosophical relativism, ontological or semantic.

It is hard to see how anyone can reject the very general thesis of cultural relativism, although it is entirely possible to disagree about its extent or scope. As for semantic relativism, I hope I have said enough in the preceding chapters, especially in chapter 7, to make it unnecessary for me to dwell at length on its merits or defects. I have taken the view that the full meaning of an utterance, or of what Austin called a 'total speech-act in a total speech-situation', is determined by discovering what speech-act is being performed by the speaker on a given occasion of utterance. Speech-acts, like acts in general, presuppose a cultural and contextual framework. Whether someone is praying, for instance, when he says 'Hallowed be thy name!' or merely uttering words in an incoherent way, cannot be determined without finding out what uses, if any, expressions such as the above are put to in, say, Christianity; whether the speaker is in church or in a sauna; whether the tone of his voice is deferential or mocking. But equally, in any given way of life, only certain expressions are conventionally used to perform certain speech-acts, because only these have the particular meanings that are deemed appropriate for the performance of those acts. Meaning, therefore, is jointly determined by the conventional role assigned to an expression in a given form of life *and* the normal, shall we say, 'dictionary' sense that it has in the natural language in question. Looked at this way, semantic relativism may seem not to be in competition with, but rather complementary to, semantic realism. Whether 'God loves men' constitutes an ordinary assertion, or an act of praising, praying, exalting, reassuring, etc, is, of course, dependent on the universe of discourse; but if it is an assertion, then it should satisfy some assertability conditions, even if these can only be deciphered by looking at the form of life in question. Extreme semantic relativism, that is, the view that meaning is entirely a function of theory or form of life – without regard to the normal, dictionary sense of an expression and what role(s) it typically plays, and why, in determining the sense of sentences in which it occurs – is, in my opinion, false because it has absurd consequences. Among other things, it makes it difficult to give an intelligible account of language-learning. On a realist analysis, a child may start learning by first simply mimicking sentences and seeing what happens. But gradually he progresses to analysing them into component expressions and noting what contributions they make to the sense of other sentences in which they occur and what usually happen to be the assertability conditions of the latter. This account does justice to the view that a child's learning must, after an initial period of mimicking, etc., be governed by rules and principles, rather than by the outcome of unending enumerative learning of every single sentence in the language. It should be noted that a child, say, in a Christian culture, not only learns to discriminate when it may be appropriate or inappropriate to say 'God is in heaven', etc by observing the behaviour of his peers: an inquisitive child learns also by asking, 'What does God look like?', 'Can God be seen?', 'But does God *really* exist?', and the like. The latter set of questions seem to me to be indicative of the child's initiation into considerations of assertability conditions, truth-conditions, and the like, albeit in a rudimentary way. I have here no doubt oversimplified the issues underlying the choice between semantic realism and relativism. But, then, the present context does not permit a discussion of all the complexity. So I must now move on to ontological relativism.

Ontological relativism denies that there is such a thing as an 'objective reality', existing, and knowable, independently of theories, conceptual frameworks and forms of life. The reality/unreality of an entity is not a question that can, or should, be answered except within the framework of the theory which postulates it, or otherwise makes use of it. This central platform commits the relativist to certain well-known positions on epistemological and logical issues. Unlike the realist, who normally espouses some kind of correspondence theory and for whom a (declarative) sentence is true or false depending on how the 'world' is, the relativist regards the truth or falsity of a sentence as being determined by its coherence or otherwise with a given theory, there being (for him) no such thing as a 'world' independent of theory. In keeping with this view, the relativist holds that the same sentence can be true in one theory but false in another. He thus disputes the realist view that the Law of Excluded Middle holds and that, therefore, a given sentence must be either true or false, *although in any given case we may not be able to find out exactly which*. For a realist the actual truth or falsity of a sentence is quite independent of the universe of discourse, or relevant theory. A certain theory may well demand that a sentence be construed as true, but that does not guarantee that it may not actually be false. For a relativist, on the other hand, there is no such distinction to be drawn here. Finally, for the relativist, there cannot be a rational choice between belief-systems, something a realist insists on.

We started this chapter with the defence of what can now be

recognised as the realist position regarding the choice between competing belief-systems. I will, therefore, refrain from saying more on that subject, except to return to it briefly towards the end of the chapter. The other issues must be joined now. Since these, however, constitute one of the main recurring themes of recent analytic philosophy, their complexity cannot adequately be captured here, nor is this the proper place to do so. We will, therefore, only look at them as they relate to religion. Let us start with what at least looks like a glaring paradox in relation to the central issue between ontological realism and relativism. Each religion seems to assume that there is a body of truths, or a reality, which, while it *happens* to be captured by that religion, is in fact quite independent of the system itself. Religious traditions do not generally entertain the possibility that the transcendental reality they all speak of is in any sense brought into being by the belief-systems concerned: this reality exists quite independently of the beliefs; there is a 'world' independent of the theories. On the other hand, however, a non-believer certainly notices, and even the believer must at least occasionally note, that there are many different religions and hence many different descriptions of reality, each claimed to be true by the relevant religion; and, what is more, none generally prepared to allow its claims to be assessed either by 'secular' criteria or by those of another religion.

The traditional 'solution' to this paradox – not that religion itself need have seen it that way – has been to regard one's own religion to be true and the others false and superstitious. This is quite consistent with the realist premise of religions: the Law of Excluded Middle holds, and hence if one's own religion describes reality truly, the others must be false. The question that interests me, however, is whether there is another, more satisfactory, solution to the paradox. Is it possible to reconcile ontological realism with some moderate form of relativism? On the face of it, surely the answer can only be 'no'. I like to think, however, that if due notice is taken of what may or may not be strictly entailed by ontological realism, then a version of it can be developed which might well be able to accommodate a moderate form of relativism. In what follows that is the task I try to accomplish.

We noted above that while realism must believe that the truth or falsity of a sentence is determined by whether or not the states of affairs which make it so obtain – for realism states of affairs, events, entities, etc exist independently of theory – it cannot, and does not, insist that on any given occasion one necessarily *knows* whether the state of affairs in question actually obtains. It is primarily for this reason, I would have thought, that Popper views the progress of science in terms of conjectures and refutations. The business of science is to discover reality, but reality is not an open book which can be read out at a glance. Hence the scientist makes conjectures or hypotheses and then sets out to falsify them, hoping all the time that if his conjecture does portray reality, its truth will be vindicated. It is possible on this view to have many competing conjectures or theories – each claiming to describe nature more truly than the others – whose actual truth or falsity can only be demonstrated in due course. Just as nature determines which species is fit to survive the struggle for life, so reality will 'select' the theory that describes it truly, or approximates its complexity more closely. Meanwhile, attempted falsifications of these theories must go on. Nature will ultimately ensure the survival of the theory that deserves to be retained, the others being discarded as false or inadequate.

This supposition, *if treated as a methodological proposal*, represents a very healthy approach to the task of the acquisition of knowledge, and therein lies the great appeal of Popper's account. Does it have any lessons for religion? I believe it does, especially if one important amendment is made. The many competing religions can all be seen as alternative descriptions of reality, no particular one of which is *known* to be true. What needs to be, and can safely be, added is the assumption that reality may be so complex that each one of these religious systems may represent a partial insight into it. Particular beliefs and practices in any of these systems may be abandoned, as they are, as a result of the growth of knowledge overall, but no single system need, although it might, be rejected altogether. The tough, stark evolutionary approach could be replaced by a milder – and not for that reason self-evidently mistaken – one. Criticism and assessment of these belief-systems in general, rational, terms could then be considered not only possible, but essential; for the assumption is that they all describe the same reality which itself exists quite independently of human conceptualisations. This '*methodological* realism', as I would like to call it, does justice to the 'realistic premise' of religion; it places religion firmly alongside other spheres of human rational activity rather than treats it as an oddity; it captures the recurring note of agnosticism and mystery found in all religions; and, while not making reality a human construct, still leaves room for a moderate form of relativism. The

*Rig Veda* declared, at least three thousand years ago, 'Truth is one but sages call it by different names',[3] and the Jains later developed it into a fully-fledged philosophical doctrine, called '*anekāntavāda*'[4] or the manysidedness of reality. The parable of the seven blind men and the elephant is often brought in to illustrate this doctrine. Depending on which part of the elephant one of the blind men touches, he describes it as either a 'serpent', a 'winnowing fan', a 'banana plant', or the like. While each one of these represents a true partial description of reality, the elephant as a whole is not truly described by any of them. For us even to be able to say that this or that is a partial description of reality, we need to assume that there is an objective reality to be described, which may perhaps be only perceived in its wholeness by a wise, omniscient being, a Yogin or a liberated man. The Jaina doctrine, however, rapidly degenerated into an unhealthy relativism, making it impossible to assert anything whatsoever categorically. The methodological realism I have suggested merely eliminates dogmatism, without making religious discourse immune to criticism; while the truth or falsity of particular metaphysical propositions occurring in religious discourse may be indeterminate, and indeterminable, at a given time, the principle that sooner or later, through normal or extraordinary perception, their truth or falsity can be discovered, is preserved.

This is why criticism and assessment – internal and external – of religious claims is important. The need to see to what extent a religious belief-system is consistent; to what extent it can accommodate scientific facts and cogent philosophical reasoning; whether the morals incorporated in it are socially cohesive or disruptive in the larger context of mankind; whether its outlook allows caring and consideration for all forms of life and not just for humanity or narrow sections of it – all these could, and should, serve as legitimate criteria for the assessment of religious systems. Those religions that are found wanting on one or more of these criteria may eventually pay the price of diminished ranks and empty pulpits. Conscious choice between rival religions may at present be rather the exception than the rule, but in principle, the situation could reverse itself.

Whatever else may or may not happen, though, one outcome seems very likely. After all the criteria of consistency, moral tone, 'truth-productivity', etc have been applied, choice in the context of religion, it seems to me, will still in the end remain the individual's *personal* one. Since there is no ideology or mechanism in the field of religion which could ensure the rejection of whole theories – indeed, as I suggested, the opposite might be the case – the choice of retention or rejection of a belief system may be exercised by an individual, in the light of his personal needs and his judgment of whether it is adequate for his purposes. And this, in a way, is as it ought to be. For religion, in my opinion, does originate in a personal 'blik'; and it is only to be expected that the rejection of religious belief should be caused, if and when it is, by the undermining or destruction of this 'blik'. But this 'undermining' of either the 'blik' itself or of the metaphysical theory supporting it would on the whole be a result of rational enquiry, criticism and assessment. Claims of fideism notwithstanding, religion, it seems to me, is basically a rational enterprise, governed by rules which may be unstated but which are there none the less.

# Notes

CHAPTER 1

1. Frank P. Ramsey, *The Foundations of Mathematics* (London, 1965) Epilogue, p. 287.
2. Ibid., pp. 288–9.
3. A useful collection of such definitions is to be found in William P. Alston, 'Religion', in *The Encyclopedia of Philosophy*, Paul Edwards (ed.) (London, 1967) vol. 7, p. 140; from which are taken all the definitions discussed here.
4. D. Z. Phillips, *Religion Without Explanation* (Oxford, 1976) p. 86.

CHAPTER 2

1. Norman Malcolm, 'Anselm's Ontological Arguments', *Philosophical Review*, vol. LXIX, no. 1 (January 1960) pp. 41–62.
2. Alvin Plantinga, *God, Freedom and Evil* (London, 1975) p. 112.
3. David Hume, *Dialogues Concerning Natural Religion*, N. Kemp Smith (ed.) (Edinburgh, 1947); *An Enquiry Concerning Human Understanding*, Selby-Bigge (ed.) (Oxford, 1975).
4. William Craig, *The Kalām Cosmological Argument* (London, 1979).
5. The debate on the BBC, 1948, is reprinted in *A Modern Introduction to Philosophy*, Paul Edwards and Arthur Pap (eds.) (New York, 1965) pp. 473–90.
6. Craig, op. cit., p. 63.
7. J. N. Findlay, 'Can God's Existence be Disproved?' in *New Essays in Philosophical Theology*, Anthony Flew and Alasdair MacIntyre (eds.) (London, 1969) pp. 47–56.
8. George Hughes, 'Can God's Existence be Disproved?', op. cit., pp. 56–67.
9. Anthony Flew, 'Theology and Falsification' in *New Essays in Philosophical Theology*, op. cit., pp. 96–9.
10. Kai Nielsen, *Contemporary Critiques of Religion* (London, 1971) p. 114.
11. Richard Swinburne, *The Coherence of Theism* (Oxford, 1977).
12. Paul Ziff, 'About God' in *Religious Experience and Truth*, Sydney Hook (ed.) (New York, 1961) pp. 195–202.
13. Ibid., p. 202.
14. See Mircea Eliade, *From Primitives to Zen* (London, 1977) Ch. 1.

CHAPTER 3

1. Friedrich Waismann, 'Verifiability' in *Logic and Language*, 1st Series, Anthony Flew (ed.) (Oxford, 1963) p. 119.

2. Ibid.
3. For an outline of the kind of case that could be made for humanism and Marxism to be counted as religions, see, for example, Ninian Smart, *The Philosophy of Religion* (New York, 1970) Ch. 1; and *The Religious Experience of Mankind* (New York, 1977), especially Chs. 1 and 10.
4. Waismann, op. cit., p. 122.
5. In previous chapters we have already made various references to Ayer and Flew who, among others, have argued in this fashion.
6. The 'sameness', in so far as it is obtainable, is meant to refer to the factual contents, if any, of the experience only, for in a psychological, subjective, sense each experience is unique and private to an individual; and no one else may be said to have it.
7. R. M. Hare, 'Theology and Falsification' in *New Essays in Philosophical Theology*, Anthony Flew and Alasdair MacIntyre (eds.) (London, 1969) pp. 99–103.
8. Shivesh Thakur, 'Conjecture and Criticism in Religious Belief', *Religious Studies*, vol. 15 (1979) pp. 71–8.

CHAPTER 4

1. William P. Alston, 'Religion' in *The Encyclopedia of Philosophy*, Paul Edwards (ed.) (New York, 1967) vol. 7, pp. 140–5.
2. Ninian Smart, *The Religious Experience of Mankind* (New York, 1977) pp. 15–25.
3. For a defence of the possibility of definition for 'cluster concepts' and for an account of what the author calls 'sufficiency definitions', see David Cooper, 'Definitions and "Clusters"', *Mind*, vol. LXXXI, N.S., No. 324 (1972) pp. 495–503.
4. John Hick, 'Religious Faith as Experiencing-As' in *Talk of God*, G. N. A. Vesey (ed.) (London, 1969) pp. 20–35.
5. Ibid., p. 23.
6. Alston, op. cit.
7. W. Cantwell Smith, *The Meaning and End of Religion* (New York, 1966); and *Questions of Religious Truth* (New York, 1967).
8. Ninian Smart, *The Science of Religion and the Sociology of Knowledge* (Princeton, 1973) pp. 55–6.
9. *Rigveda*, Mandala x, Hymn 121, in *The Hymns of the Rigveda*, R. T. H. Griffith (ed. and trans.) (Benares, 1920–6) vol. II.
10. *Rigveda*, Mandala x, Hymn 129, in *Hymns from the Rigveda*, A. A. Macdonell (ed. and trans.) (London, 1922).

CHAPTER 5

1. This thesis could be disputed for very different sets of reasons, some of which will be discussed in the rest of the book, especially chapters 7–10. One of them, probably unlikely to be so discussed, at least directly, is offered by John Hick in an unpublished comment. 'I would myself', he writes, 'not say that religion explains, but that theology explains, religion being basically religious

experience, religious worship and religious life, and theology consisting of a set of metaphysical theories to explain the data of experience.' I do not disagree with his view that theology explains, but its explanatory function presupposes, in my opinion, the general explanatory character of religious belief-systems. As I see it, the world as viewed through religious experience is explained by the metaphysical theory of a given religion and the relevant theology tries to explain problems and paradoxes generated by the theory. The detailed contents of this chapter will, I hope, show convincingly why religious systems ought to be treated as explanatory theories.
2. This model, much discussed by philosophers of science, is particularly elegantly formulated and defended by Carl Hempel. See, for example, Carl Hempel and Paul Oppenheim, 'Studies in the Logic of Explanation', *Philosophy of Science*, xv, 1948; reprinted, among other places, in *Readings in the Philosophy of Science*, Baruch A. Brody (ed.) (Englewood Cliffs, N.J., 1970) pp. 8–28. Part 1 of this book, entitled 'Explanation and Prediction: Goals of the Scientific Enterprise', includes articles on the subject by many well-known philosophers of science, e.g. Ayer, Braithwaite, Nagel, Scriven, and others.
3. Michael Scriven, 'Explanations of the Supernatural' in *Philosophy and Psychical Research*, Shivesh Thakur (ed.) (London, 1976) p. 194.
4. Ludwig Wittgenstein, Review of Frazer's *The Golden Bough*, *Synthese*, 17, 1967.
5. See Hempel and Oppenheim, 'Studies in the Logic of Explanation' in *Readings in the Philosophy of Science*, op. cit., especially pp. 11–12.
6. For a detailed critique of the claim of identity between explanation and prediction, see, for example, Michael Scriven, 'Explanations, Predictions and Laws' in *Minnesota Studies in the Philosophy of Science*, Herbert Feigl and Grover Maxwell (eds.) (Minneapolis, 1962) vol. 3.

CHAPTER 6

1. D. Z. Phillips, *Faith and Philosophical Enquiry* (London, 1970) p. 30; and elsewhere.
2. Richard Popkin, 'Fideism' in *The Encyclopedia of Philosophy*, Paul Edwards (ed.) (London, 1967) vol. 3, pp. 201–2; see also his 'Theological and Religious Scepticism', *The Christian Scholar*, vol. 39 (1956) pp. 150–8.
3. David Hume, *An Essay Concerning Human Understanding*, L. A. Selby-Bigge (ed.) (Oxford, 1951) p. 131.
4. Sören Kierkegaard, *Philosophical Fragments, Or A Fragment of Philosophy*, David Swenson (trans.) (Princeton, 1946).
5. Popkin (1967), op. cit.
6. Gilbert Ryle, *The Concept of Mind* (London, 1968).
7. Kai Nielsen, 'Wittgensteinian Fideism', *Philosophy*, vol. XLII, no. 161 (July 1967) pp. 191–209.
8. Peter Winch, *The Idea Of A Social Science* (London, 1958); and 'Understanding A Primitive Society' in *Religion and Understanding*, D. Z. Phillips (ed.) (Oxford, 1967) pp. 9–42.
9. Winch (1958), op. cit., p. 110.
10. Ibid., p. 109.
11. Ibid., pp. 100–1.

12. Shivesh Thakur, Review of Phillips' *Faith and Philosophical Enquiry*, in *Australasian Journal of Philosophy*, vol. 49, no. 3 (December 1971) pp. 324-9.

CHAPTER 7

1. Alfred J. Ayer, *Language, Truth and Logic* (London, 1970).
2. Anthony Flew, 'Theology and Falsification', op. cit.
3. C. B. Martin, *Religious Belief* (New York, 1959).
4. John Wisdom, 'Gods', reprinted in *Philosophy and Psychoanalysis* (Oxford, 1953); 'The Logic of God', and 'Religious Belief', reprinted in *Paradox and Discovery* (Oxford, 1965).
5. R. B. Braithwaite, *An Empiricist's View of the Nature of Religious Belief* (Cambridge, 1955), as reprinted in *Philosophy of Religion: A Book of Readings*, G. K. Abernathy and T. A. Langford (eds.) (New York, 1962).
6. Ibid., p. 376.
7. Ibid., p. 378.
8. Ibid., pp. 380–1.
9. Kai Nielsen (1967), op. cit.
10. D. Z. Phillips, *The Concept of Prayer* (London, 1965); *Faith and Philosophical Enquiry* (London, 1970).
11. Shivesh Thakur, Review of Phillips' *Faith and Philosophical Enquiry*, op. cit.
12. Ibid.
13. St Thomas Aquinas, *Summa Theologica*, Part 1, Question XIII. For a lucid but brief account of this doctrine, see John Hick, *Philosophy of Religion* (New Jersey, 1963) Chapter 6.
14. I. T. Ramsey, *Religious Language* (London, 1957); *Models and Mystery* (Oxford, 1964).
15. Paul Tillich, *Systematic Theology* (Chicago, 1951–1963); *The Dynamics of Faith* (New York, 1957).
16. J. L. Austin, *How to Do Things with Words* (Oxford, 1971).
17. John R. Searle, *Speech Acts* (Cambridge, 1970).
18. See P. F. Strawson, 'Truth', *Analysis*, IX, no. 6 (1949) and 'Truth', *P.A.S.* suppl. vol. XXIV (1950).
19. J. L. Austin, op. cit., pp. 150–63.

CHAPTER 8

1. D. Z. Phillips, *Religion Without Explanation* (Oxford, 1976) Ch. 7, p. 100. Space does not permit a discussion of the details of his argument in this chapter; but it follows familiar Wittgensteinian lines.
2. A. S. Eddington, *The Nature of the Physical World* (Cambridge, 1928).
3. John Skorupski, *Symbol and Theory* (Cambridge, 1976).
4. E. E. Evans-Pritchard, *Theories of Primitive Religion* (Oxford, 1977), p. 15.
5. Ibid., p. 6.
6. Ibid., p. 26.
7. Ibid.

8. Ibid.
9. Ibid., see pages 5, 32, 53.
10. Skorupski, op. cit., p. 180.
11. Ibid., p. 189.
12. Ibid., pp. 194–200.
13. H. L. Bergson, *The Two Sources of Morality and Religion* (New York, 1935).

CHAPTER 9

1. Karl R. Popper, *Conjectures and Refutations* (London, 1963); and *Logic of Scientific Discovery* (London, 1959).
2. S. C. Thakur, 'Popper on Scientific Method', *Philosophical Studies*, vol. XIX (1970) pp. 71–82.
3. E. B. Tylor, *Primitive Culture* (London, 1891); see also John Skorupski's discussion of Tylor's 'blocks to falsifiability' in *Symbol and Theory*, op. cit., pp. 4–7. For a discussion of a similar, although not identical, set of points made by Evans-Pritchard, see Peter Winch, 'Understanding a Primitive Society', op. cit., especially Part I.
4. Skorupski, op. cit., pp. 7–8.
5. See *The Myth of God Incarnate*, John Hick (ed.) (London, 1977).
6. S. C. Thakur, Review of Phillips' *Faith and Philosophical Enquiry*, op. cit.
7. T. S. Kuhn, *The Structure of Scientific Revolutions* (London, 1975).

CHAPTER 10

1. T. S. Kuhn, *The Structure of Scientific Revolutions*, op. cit.
2. The realism–relativism controversy pervades a great deal of contemporary philosophy – in metaphysics and epistemology, in philosophy of science and philosophical logic, and is the theme of many of the works of Quine, Goodman, Feyerabend, Frege, Popper, Dummett and Davidson, to name only a few. For a discussion of some of the issues involved, especially in the context of religion, see John Skorupski, *Symbol and Theory*, op. cit., Appendix, pp. 225–43.
3. *Rigveda*, Griffith (ed.), *op. cit.*, Mandala I, Hymn 164.
4. For an authoritative account of the philosophy of Jainism, see S. N. Dasgupta, *A History of Indian Philosophy* (Cambridge, 1969) vol. I.

# Index

N.B. References to the Notes (pp. 116–20) are given in the form: 119:8, that is, notes to Chapter 8, on page 119.

Action-commitments, see Religion
Alston, W. P., 35–8, 41, 116:1
Anselm, 11–12
Aquinas, see Thomas Aquinas
Aristotle, 43
Arnold, M., 29
Attitude-commitments, see Religion
Austin, J. L., 78, 81, 110
Ayer, A. J., 70

Belief-commitments, see Religion
Bergson, H. L., 94
Bliks, see Religion
Bradley, F. H., 5–6
Braithwaite, R. B., 72–4

Caird, E., 6
Cantwell Smith, W., 42
Cooper, D. E., 117:4
Cosmological argument, see God
Craig, W. L., 14–15

Dasgupta, S. N., 120:10
Deductive-nomological model, see Scientific explanation
Descartes, R., 15
Design, argument from, see God

Eddington, A. S., 87
Eliade, M., 116:2
Evans-Pritchard, E. E., 88–9, 120:9
Experience, see Religion
Experiencing-as, see Religion
Explanation, see Religion, and Scientific explanation

Faith, see Religion
Falsifiability, see Religious claims
Feuerbach, L., 7
Fideism, 2, 62ff., 74–6, 80, 95–6, 100–1
Findlay, J. N., 15–17
Flew, A. G. N., 17–18, 70, 95
Forms of life, 65–9, 74–6, 80
Frazer, J., 90, 91

God:
   Arguments against existence, 15–19
   Arguments for existence, 10–15
      Cosmological, 14–15
      Design, 13–14
      Ontological, 11–13, 17

Hare, R. M., 26, 72
Hempel, C., 118:5
Hick, J., 39, 117–18:5
Horton, W. R. G., 88, 91–4
Hughes, G., 16–17
Humanism, 23
Hume, D., 7, 13, 34, 43, 62, 70
Hypothetico-deductive model, see Scientific explanation

Ineffability, see Religion

Kant, I., 11, 12, 13
Kierkegaard, S., 62
Kuhn, T. S., 93, 101, 105

Language games, 74–5
Linguistic philosophy, 1

MacIntyre, A., 100–1

# Index

McTaggart, J. M. E., 6
Magic, 88–94
Malcolm, N., 11–13
Martin, C. B., 70
Martineau, J., 5
Marxism, 23
Metaphysics, 1, 24–5, 34, 72, 83–8, 96–7, *see also* Religion
Morality, *see* Religion

Nielsen, K., 18, 65, 74

Ontological argument, *see* God
Otto, R., 6

Personal experience, *see* Religion
Phillips, D. Z., 6–7, 60ff., 75–6, 100–1, 119:8
Plantinga, A., 13
Popkin, R. H., 118:6
Popper, K. R., 96–7, 105, 113
Positivism, 1, 2
Prediction, *see* Religion, *and* Scientific explanation
Prescriptivism, 4–5, 33–4
Primitive societies, 90–4, 97–8
Pseudo-science, *see* Religion

Ramsey, F. P., 1–2
Ramsey, I. T., 76–7
Realism and relativism:
  Cultural, 109–10
  Ontological, 108–9, 111–12
  Semantic, 109–11
Reductionism, 2, 5, 6–7, 33, 88–9
Religion:
  As action-commitments, 29, 30–1, 36–7, 78
  As attitude-commitments, 29–30, 36–7, 78
  As belief-commitments, 29–30, 78
  As experiencing-as, 39
  As explanation, 47–59, 83–94, 101–4, 117–18:5
  As ineffable, 2–3
  As metaphysics, 22–9, 32, 34, 35–6, 38, 72, 78, 83–8, 94, 95, 96–7
  As morality, 31–2, 36–7

As personal experience (bliks), 25–9, 32, 37–8, 39, 40, 44, 48–9, 58, 115
  As prediction, 56–9, 92–4, 97–8
  As pre-scientific, 56–7, 83, 88–94
  As pseudo-science, 50–9, 88–94, 97–8, 102
  As social activity, 36, 40–43
Religious belief, rejection, 95–104, 106–7, 115
Religious claims, testability, 53–6, 95, 96, 101–4
Religious language, 57, 65–6, 70–82, 84–6, 95
Russell, B., 14, 39
Ryle, G., 64

Scientific explanation, 50–9, 63, 96–7, 102, 105–8
  Deductive-nomological (hypothetico-deductive) model, 51–3, 58
  Prediction, 58–9
Scriven, M., 55–6, 118:5
Searle, J. R., 78
Skorupski, J., 88, 98, 120:10
Smart, N., 35, 41, 42, 117:3
Social anthropology, 88–94
Speech acts, 78–92, 109–10
Spencer, H., 5
Strawson, P. F., 119:7
Swinburne, R., 18

Testability, *see* Religious claims
Thakur, S. C., 31, 69, 75–6, 97, 101
Theocentrism, 5, 10–11, 19–20, 33
Thomas Aquinas, 10, 16, 76–7
Tiele, C. P., 6
Tillich, P., 76
Tylor, E. B., 89–90, 91, 97–8, 101

Verifiability, *see* Religious claims

Waismann, F., 22, 116–17:3
Winch, P., 66–8, 120:9
Wisdom, J., 71–2
Wittgenstein, L., 1, 21, 56, 65, 76, 77

Ziff, P., 18